Hitler's Raketen U-Boote

(Rocket Submarines)

The True Story of the Steinhoff Brothers
and the
Nazi's First Submarine Launched Missiles

The Untold New England
U-Boat Saga & Murder Mystery

Paul M. Lawton, Esquire
Naval Historian

Dedication

This story is dedicated to the brave, young men and women who fought and sacrificed on both sides during World War II. To the brothers, Kapitanleutnant Friedrich and Dr. Ernst Steinhoff; to my late uncle, U.S. Army (M4 Sherman) tank commander, Lieutenant John Henry Cashman, Jr. ("H" Company, 1st Armored Regiment, 1st Armored Division), who was killed in action at the Battle for Hill 609 in Tunisia, North Africa during "Operation Vulcan" on Friday 30 April 1943; and to my late father, Judge (Ret.) James Robert Lawton (10/20/1925 - 03/20/2007), formerly deployed with "I" Company, 503rd Parachute Infantry Regiment, 17th Airborne Division, U.S. Army, who was seriously wounded in action by a German Panther tank shell at the outskirts of Wessel, Germany during "Operation Varsity" on Friday 30 March 1945, who got me interested in the research of military history.

Contents

Front Cover Photographs

Right: Kapitanleutnant Friedrich Steinhoff, Commander of the Type IXD-2 German U-boat, *U-873* after surrendering his boat. Taken on Wednesday, May 17, 1945 at the Portsmouth (New Hampshire) U.S. Navy Base. Steinhoff is seen under U.S. Marine armed guard before being transferred by bus to Boston (Photograph courtesy of Clint Winslow, former Officer aboard the U.S. Coast Guard Cutter USCGC *Argo*).

Center: The submerged Type IXC U-boat *U-511* under command of Kapitanleutnant Friedrich Steinhoff, conducting the first successful submerged test launch of Wurfkorper 24 Speng (Rocket, Model 42) German Army artillery rockets, off the coast of Germany's secret rocket test center at Peenemunde, on the Baltic Sea, on June 4, 1942. (Courtesy of the late Horst Bredow, Curator at the U-Boot-Archiv at Cuxhaven-Altenbruch, Germany).

Right: Doctor Ernst A. Steinhoff circa 1970 while working as Chief Scientist of the Air Force Missile Development Center at Holloman Air Force Base. He later served an extended term as Director of the New Mexico Research Institute. He passed away on Wednesday, December 2nd 1987 (Courtesy of Monika Steinhoff-O'Friel).

Back Cover Photograph

Kapitanleutnant Friedrich Steinhoff and his Officers and crewmen mustered aboard the U-boat, *U-873* at the AG Weser shipyard at Bremen, Germany, upon her Commissioning on March 1, 1944. (Courtesy of Dr. Frank Steinhoff)

Hitler's Raketen U-Boote
(Rocket Submarines)

*The True Story of the Steinhoff Brothers
and the
Nazi's First Submarine Launched Missiles*

*The Untold New England
U-Boat Saga & Murder Mystery*

During World War II, two German brothers, one a submarine Commander and the other a rocket scientist, merged their respective areas of expertise into the development of a weapons system that would change military history and set the stage for a new balance of world military and political power. Their visionary work on the development of submarine-launched rockets placed the United States military in fear of an attack against New York City, not unlike that which took place nearly six decades later, on September 11, 2001. Tragically, one brother died under mysterious circumstances as a prisoner of war in the custody of U.S. military authorities, while the other went on to become one of the chief architects of America's ballistic missile and space programs, helping to win the Cold War for NATO and all free nations, against the spread of world Communism.

The Steinhoff Brothers

Ernst August Steinhoff was born the son of Ludwig Steinhoff, a civil servant, and his wife Augusta Steinhoff in Treysa, Germany on February 11, 1908. During the late 1920s and 1930s, as a young man, Ernst became involved in Germany's then popular rocketry and aviation clubs, where his interest in physics, flight mechanics and electronics shaped the direction of his future career aspirations. Ernst Steinhoff went on to receive his Master of Science degree, summa cum laude, and his Doctor of Engineering degree, cum laude, from the Darmstadt Institute of Technology in Darmstadt, Germany. In 1935 Dr. Steinhoff married Hildegard Madee, and they had seven children. In 1935 Dr. Ernst Steinhoff set the world's record for solo long distance cross-country sail-plane (glider) flight of 314 miles, after which he was bestowed the honorary rank of "Flight Captain" with the German air force (Luftwaffe) for his flight achievements. Dr. Steinhoff taught aeronautical engineering at the Polytechnic Institute, Bad Frankenhausen, Germany, from 1936 to 1939, and conducted experimental work in aerodynamics, flight mechanics and airborne electronics equipment at the Aeronautical Research Institute at Darmstadt, Germany. He later became Director of Flight Mechanics, Ballistics, Guidance and Control and Instrumentation at the secret German Rocket Research Center at Peenamunde, Germany, on the Ostsee (Baltic Sea) coast, where he served from July 1st 1939 to the Spring of 1945.

The second Steinhoff son, Friedrich, was born on July 14, 1909 in the village of Kullstedt in Thuringen, Germany, followed by a third brother, Ludwig II, who was born in 1912. In his early 20s Friedrich Steinhoff served in the German Merchant Marine before entering as an Officer-cadet in the Seaman Branch of the Kriegsmarine (W.W. II era German Navy), with the Class of 1935. He served with the 4th Minesweeper Flotilla until May of 1940[1], then was assigned to the Coastal Defense Group at Bergen, Norway, where he served until March of 1941. He underwent U-boat training from March of 1941 to July of 1941, before being assigned as a Wach Offizier (Watch Officer), for sea trials aboard the German Type VIIC U-boat, *U-96* under command of Kapitanleutnant (Lieutenant Commander) Heinrich Lehmann-Willenbrock, where he served until November of 1941. On December 1, 1941 he was promoted to Kapitanleutnant (Lieutenant Commander), and on December 8, 1941 he assumed command of the Type IXC U-boat, *U-511*.

Kapitanleutnant Steinhoff was married to Ilse Steinhoff on July 22, 1939, and they had three sons, the oldest of whom, Dirk, was born in 1940 but died of diphtheria at just three years of age. The Steinhoffs' second son, Frank, was born in Cuxhaven on February 19, 1942, and their youngest son, Joern, was born on May 29, 1945, two months after Commander Steinhoff sailed from Germany on his last war patrol.

The Steinhoffs were a tight-knit family, and because of their proximity in age, Ernst and Friedrich in particular, remained very close throughout their lives, as Ernst pursued his prominent career in aviation, and as Friedrich rose through the ranks in the maritime and naval services. The Steinhoff brothers were well educated and highly motivated young men, and were respected and admired by their peers and subordinates as they excelled through their respective careers. As World War II drew closer, their knowledge and leadership qualities became a coveted commodity to the German war effort, and their combined knowledge and experience would ultimately change world history in a way that they could hardly, at that time, have imagined.

Few aside from Kapitanleutnant Friedrich Steinhoff's wife Ilse, knew that he had preferred service in the surface fleet, but that he had been impressed into the U-boat arm of the Kriegsmarine. According to Ilse Steinhoff, "he [Friedrich] loved the sea but he loved the fresh air and the wide view of the horizon. He feared the narrowness and the smell of the submerged submarine." By all accounts he was worshiped by his young Officers and crewmen, for his skilled seamanship, easy-going temperament, fairness and concern for their safety and well being during those long and dangerous combat patrols.

During the war years Adolf Hitler's Third Reich spent billions of Reichsmarks and vast resources on the research, development and procurement of many new, highly advanced weapons systems, several of which would change the nature of future land, sea and air warfare. From guided missiles, to tanks, submarines, heavy artillery, small arms and high performance aircraft, Germany's top scientists, engineers and technicians were impressed into the various armaments industries for the purpose of creating the most technologically advanced military power in the world to that time. Military personnel and technically trained civilians were encouraged to support the war effort, and to volunteer their ideas that might better outfit Germany's Wehrmacht (armed forces), for battle.

The Birth of Submarine-Launched Rockets

During 1941, Kapitanleutnant Steinhoff had consulted occasionally with his brother, Doktor (Doctor) Ernst Steinhoff, then a scientist and engineer working on rocket guidance and telemetry systems at the secret German Army's experimental rocket test center (Versuchsstelle) at Peenemunde on the Baltic Sea coast. Merging their respective areas of training, the Steinhoff brothers discussed the possibility of arming U-boats with rocket launchers capable of attacking Allied port facilities, military and industrial installations, coastal defenses and convoys. The most technically challenging requirement for the development of such a weapon system, however, was the capability of launching the U-boat's rockets while submerged. Both men proposed the idea to their respective superiors seeking seed money for a research prototype, and initially their idea was received with a degree of optimism. Commander Steinhoff presented the idea to Grossadmiral Karl Dönitz, Commander-in-Chief of the Kriegsmarine's U-boat service, suggesting potential American coastal targets, stating: "With this device I can blast any harbor—or any shore target—from positions miles out at sea." Dr. Ernst Steinhoff presented the idea to Peenemunde's Technische Direktor (Technical Director), Doktor (Dr.) Wernher von Braun, who agreed that: "If a rocket can work in space, it can work in water."

In May of 1942 the Steinhoff brothers and a team of German scientists under the guidance of Dr. von Braun, began the design and development of such a weapon at Peenemunde under the designation Projekt "Ursel" (a few otherwise credible sources on U-boats and their weapons systems erroneously described Ursel as a project for development of U-boat launched anti-aircraft and anti-surface-ship missiles). The German Army, rather than Air-Force "Luftwaffe," was in control of the Peenemunde rocket research facility because German military planners believed rocketry was simply the logical progression from artillery. The Ursel weapon prototype consisted of six (6) slightly modified, though off-the-shelf, solid propellant, roll-stabilized Nebelwerfer 42 (so-called "smoke-thrower" because of the pronounced white smoke trail they left behind in flight), 30 centimeter diameter (11.8 inch) Wurfkorper 24 Spreng, German Army issue, heavy artillery rockets manufactured by the armaments firm Rheinmetall-Borsig. Each rocket was approximately 4 feet in length, weighed 279.4 pounds including a 98.3 pound high-explosive warhead, traveled at a velocity of 754 feet per second and had a range of 4,960 yards (approximately 2.8 miles). The modified sea-launch version of the rocket was designated the "Do-38," with the abbreviation "Do" (as "Me" stands for Messerschmitt), honoring General (Dr.) Walter **Do**rnberger, the Commanding Officer of the Peenemunde research center. The Do-38 rockets were mounted in a Schweres Wurfgerat 41 launch rack which was intended to be folded flush with the U-boat's aft deck, and erected to a 45 degree firing position for launch from periscope depth (in actuality, the test launch racks were mounted in a fixed position). The first submerged test launch of the Do-38 rockets took place from a static mounted launch frame, set up by Kriegsmarine hard-hat divers on the Baltic Sea floor off the coast of Griefswalder Oie near Peenemunde, from a depth of approximately 40 feet. On June 4, 1942 the German Type IXC U-boat *U-511* commanded by Steinhoff, along with his brother, Ernst, Dr. von Braun and a group of 20 scientists, civilian technicians, German military officials, Kriegsmarine Officers and crewmen, submerged off the coast of Peenemunde, and from a depth of approximately 40 feet, launched her unguided saturation type rockets in the first successful test of such a weapon, from a submarine.[2] German propaganda newsreels of the time boasted of this great technological achievement, threatening that such weapons would soon be employed against the enemies of the Third Reich. Further development of the system ended, however, as significant performance drawbacks associated with the installation of the externally mounted launch equipment arose during testing, and because there was insufficient interest given to the project by Grossadmiral Dönitz's staff, further development of the weapon system died for lack of funding. Though the relatively small, short range Do-38 rockets developed and tested under Project "Ursel" were far from a strategic weapon system, it proved the feasibility of launching missiles from a submerged submarine. Those successful early tests would be remembered and revisited by high ranking German military officials just two years later, upon the development of far more deadly and efficient rocket systems.

There is some evidence that several German Type IIB U-boats (believed to have been the *U-9*, *U-19* & *U-24*) of the Black Sea's 30th U-Flottille based at Konstanza, Romania, fired small artillery-type rockets at Soviet forces on the coast of the Crimea in the summers of 1943 and 1944. It is believed, however, that those actions involved smaller rockets than the Do-38 test model type, possibly the longer range 15 centimeter Nebelwerfer 41 or 21cm NbW 42 rockets. One note at the end of the log of *U-18*'s (Kapitanleutnant Karl Fleige) fourth patrol during the summer of 1943 stated: "The close approach to the harbor of Poti made the bombardment with the new projectiles a total success." There are few other surviving records to shed much light on those operations, the first combat use of submarine launched missiles in naval history.

During Kapitanleutnant (KL) Steinhoff's first war patrol to

the Caribbean aboard the *U-511*, he attacked the Westbound convoy TAW-15 off Haiti on August 28, 1942. Firing three full salvos of torpedoes at three different tankers, Steinhoff remarkably struck all three, sinking the British flagged Eagle Oil & Shipping Company, Ltd. 552 foot, 13,031 ton tanker S.S. *San Fabian* at approximately 18 degrees 09 minutes North Latitude/74 degrees 38 minutes West Longitude, resulting in the loss of 26 lives, with 33 survivors rescued. The *U-511* also sank the Dutch Netherlands flagged 489 foot, 8,968 ton Petroleum Industrie Maatschappij NV Line motor-vessel M.V. *Rotterdam*, and damaged the American 484 foot, 8,773 ton Standard Oil Company of New Jersey tanker S.S. *Esso Aruba*, which limped into Guantanamo Bay, Cuba, under her own power. Refueled by the Type XIV "Milchkuh" (milk-cow) U-Boat-tanker *U-463* (Korvettenkapitan [Commander] Leo Wolfbauer) Southwest of the Azores (at which time the *U-511* transferred over a sick crewman for medical treatment), the *U-511* returned to her base at Lorient, France, where she arrived on September 29th.

On October 24, 1942 Commander Steinhoff and the U-*511* departed Lorient on her second operational combat patrol to attack Allied shipping off the South American coast. On November 8th he received orders to reverse course and head at top speed for Morocco to form up with Schlagetot (death-strike) group boats to counter "Operation Torch," the Allied invasion of North Africa. After arriving at Agadir in Southern Morocco on November 15th, Commander Steinhoff fell "ill." According to the BdU's (Befehlshaber der Unterseeboote: Commander in Chief, U-boats) war log: In the morning of 20 November 1942 the *U-511* radioed for medical assistance and on 21 November 1942, *U-155* (Type IXC under Kapitanleutnant Adolf Cornelius Piening) first met *U-511* and they then searched together for *U-118* (Type XB mine-layer converted to "Milchkuh" supply-submarine under Korvettenkapitan Werner Czygan), locating her at noon in Kriegsmarine Marinequadratkarte (German Navy chart grid-square) DH-2452, at a rendezvous point

Southeast of the Azores. While the doctor from *U-118* went aboard *U-511*, the *U-118* transferred 42m³ (42 cubic meters) of diesel fuel to the *U-155*, along with spare parts for the oil pump on her Junkers® (air) compressor, and 50 alkali (Carbon dioxide "CO_2" scrubber) cartridges, following which the *U-155* departed the scene. The *U-118*'s doctor confirmed that Steinhoff was seriously ill, and based upon his opinion that "further operations [for *U-511*] were impossible" due to her Commander's condition, she was forced to return to Lorient where she arrived on November 28th after an unsuccessful month at sea. According to *U-511*'s Stabsobermaschinist (Chief Machinist) Heinz Rehse, Commander Steinhoff was relieved of command from the *U-511* due to depression, possibly a nervous breakdown, and he was assigned to a staff position as Adjutant to the Commanding Officer (CO) at the 7th U-Flotilla headquarters at Saint-Nazaire, France (one source indicates that he was assigned to the 2nd U-Flotilla based at Lorient). The *U-511* later came under the command of Kapitanleutnant Fritz Schneewind and on March 10, 1943 sailed from Lorient for the Far East as a so-called "Monsun Group" boat "*Marco Polo I*," first to Penang, and ultimately to Kobe, Japan where she was turned over to the Imperial Japanese Navy as a gift from Adolf Hitler to Prime Minister Hideki Tojo, becoming the *RO-500*.

In March of 1944, Commander Steinhoff had recovered sufficiently to be reassigned to take command of the new long-range Type IXD-2 "U-Cruiser" U-boat, *U-873*. Built by the AG Weser shipyard at Bremen, Germany, the U-*873*'s keel was laid on February 17, 1943, she was launched on November 16, 1943 and commissioned on March 1, 1944. The *U-873* was 287 feet long, displaced 1,616 tons (1,804 tons fully loaded), and was powered by either her twin 2,200 horsepower MAN (Maschinenfabrik Augsburg-Nurnberg AG), manufactured 9-cylinder, 4-stroke M9V 40/46 supercharged compression-ignittion diesel engines, or her two 500 horsepower Siemens-Schuckert-Werke 2 GU 345/34

E-Maschine (electric motors). With expanded bunkerage to accommodate up to 510 cubic meters (442 tons) of diesel fuel oil, she had an incredible long range of 23,700 miles (while surfaced at 12 knots), and was capable of 19.2 knots surfaced, or 6.9 knots submerged. She had a standard compliment of 57 Officers and crewmen, and was armed with four bow and two stern 533 mm (21 inch) torpedo tubes for which she carried 20 torpedoes (though she was capable of carrying up to 24), including five of the most technologically advanced passive-acoustic-homing T-5s, eleven T-3s and four T-1s. The *U-873* mounted one Rheinmetall-Borsig M/42 37mm (1.46 inch) semi-automatic anti-aircraft (AA), or so-called Fliegerabwehrkanone (flak) gun on the forward deck, four Mauser C/38 20mm (.79 inch) flak guns, two each on LM43U twin mounts on platform I (the upper deck) of the "Wintergarten" (winter-garden), the raised gun platform aft of the conning tower, and a twin semi-automatic 37mm flak gun mount on platform II (the lower deck) of the Wintergarten.

After commissioning, the *U-873* sailed to Kiel where she underwent sea-trials, before transiting to Swinemunde (on the Baltic Sea), where her crew underwent *flak* (anti-aircraft gunnery) training, and then to Gotenhafen for torpedo training. During the next several months the *U-873* was dry-docked for repairs on at least three occasions after sustaining damage in collisions with two other U-boats, and after being struck by a small aerial bomb which caused considerable damage to her control-room area while she was in dry-dock on July 30, 1944. While undergoing repairs and an overhaul at Deschimag Werft at Kiel in July of 1944 the *U-873*'s auxiliary MWM 6-cylinder, RS 34.5S unsupercharged 580 horsepower diesel-powered battery charging motors and auxiliary electric generators (unique to the Type IXD-2) were removed. The *U-873* was fitted with a "schnorchel" (snorkel), and her keel duct was loaded with a strategically valuable 100 ton cargo of un-ground optical glass and mercury, as she was initially destined for a long-range voyage to

Japan. Repairs at Bremen continued through the end of November 1944 when she departed for Kiel for additional schnorcheling trials in preparation for her first patrol. After undergoing further flak practice and repairs to her auxiliary bilge pumps # 1 and # 3 at Stettin, she again transferred back to Kiel where she arrived on January 6, 1945. There, her auxiliary diesel charging motor compartment was loaded with an additional 100 tons of cargo consisting primarily of un-ground optical glass, also destined for Japan. Just days after the loading of cargo was completed, and after the arrival of 14 passengers (including several members of the Japanese diplomatic staff and German Air-Force "Luftwaffe" officials) intended to be transferred aboard the *U-873* to Japan, the orders for her first operational patrol were abruptly changed. Allegedly, because of the breakdown of diplomatic relations between Germany and Japan in the final weeks before Germany's fall, Hitler himself ordered that the *U-873* be readied for a combat patrol to sink Allied shipping in the Caribbean. Though much of her strategic cargo had been off-loaded, the 100 ton cargo of mercury and lens crystals were not removed from her keel duct, nor were her auxiliary diesel charging motors and auxiliary electric generators replaced. After transfer to Horten, Norway, and undergoing further repairs and adjustments, the *U-873* proceeded to Kristiansand, from which she departed on March 31, 1945 under command of then 35-year-old Kapitanleutnant Steinhoff, on her first, and last operational war patrol.

Historical Background

Seven months earlier, on August 20, 1944 the German Type IXC/40 U-boat, *U-1229* under command of Korvettenkapitan (KK) Armin Zinke, was located while surfaced, and was attacked with rockets and depth-bombs by a U.S. Navy Grumman TBF "Avenger" aircraft piloted by Lt. Alex X. Brokas, from the American escort carrier U.S.S. *Bogue* (*CVE-9*), approximately 300 miles East-Southeast of Cape Race, Newfoundland. The *U-1229* was forced to crash dive, though after two hours submerged and taking on water, her batteries were compromised, generating poisonous clouds of chlorine gas (chlorine gas was generated from the chemical reaction between seawater and the sulfuric acid in the U-boat's batteries). Out of power, she was forced to blow her ballast tanks to surface and ventilate. The surfaced *U-1229* immediately came under continued strafing and depth-charge attacks by six additional Avengers and Grumman F4F "Wildcat" fighter aircraft form the *Bogue*, before her pressure hull was holed, sending her to the bottom. Commander Zinke and 18 Officers and crewmen were killed in the air attack and sinking, with 42 survivors rescued by Allied warships. Among the survivors was 42-year-old "Abwehr" (German Intelligence Service) agent Oskar Mantel. Prior to the war, Mantel, a German national, had worked as a bartender in Yorkville, New York. He returned to Germany where he was trained as a spy and saboteur, and was aboard the U-*1229* to be landed at Winter Harbor, Maine.

Under interrogation by the F.B.I. and U.S. Navy Office of Naval Intelligence (ONI) personnel, Mantel attempted to appease his interrogators by telling them of rumored secret German rocket/ missile launching U-boats capable of attacking targets on the American East coast. Several other captured U-boat crewmen told their captors of Germany's newest and most advanced schnorchel fitted Type XXI electro-boats, several of which had recently been launched. Based upon this information and the earlier interrogations of German "Operation Pastorius"[3] Abwehr spies George Dasch and Ernst Berger, U.S. military intelligence became convinced that Germany's newest U-boats would soon be capable of attacking the United States with secret V-Type "Vergeltungswaffe" (Vengeance-weapons) such as the "Fieseler Fi-103" (FZG-76) Vergeltungswaffe-Eins (Vengeance-weapon One) or **"V-1"** pulse-jet powered, guided cruise-type missiles, possibly stored in water-tight, deck-mounted hangars and launched from stern mounted launch-rails[4], or Vergeltungswaffe-Zwei (Vengeance-weapon Two) or **"V-2"** (German designation "Aggregate-4" (Assembly-4) or **"A-4"**) type guided-rockets, so-called "robot bombs" similar to those laying waste to London and Antwerp, possibly to be towed in, and launched from submersible launch containers.[5]

In August of 1939, Dr. Ernst Steinhoff had become one of the early founders behind the concept of the cruise-missile, when he submitted a proposal to the Reich Air Traffic Ministry entitled "Flights at Enemy Targets with Unmanned Aircraft." According to Dr. Michael J. Neufeld, Curator of the Smithsonian Institute's National Air and Space Museum (NASM) in Washington, DC: " . . . cruise missile ideas, often called "aerial torpedoes," went back to the First World War, as indicated by Ken Warrell in *The Evolution of the Cruise Missile.*" Dr. Steinhoff's proposal to use small guided aircraft to deliver heavy warheads over long distances ultimately led to the development of the V-1 jet-powered guided-bomb, which preceded the development of the first ballistic missile, Germany's A-4/V-2 rocket. Toward the end of the war the A-4/V-2 was proving to be such a devastating weapon against London that the Supreme Allied Commander, U.S. Army General Dwight D. Eisenhower wrote that "had the V-2 been employed six months sooner, invasion of Europe would have proved exceedingly difficult, perhaps . . . impossible!"

In the Fall of 1943, a civilian of the Deutsche Arbeitsfront (German Labor Front), Direktor Otto Lafferenz, witnessed a successful test firing of an A-4/V-2 guided-rocket and suggested that the Kriegsmarine should entertain the viability of U-boats capable of launching such rockets against the American Northeast coast (some have since referred to the proposed A-4/V-2 launch vehicle as the so-called "Lafferenz capsule"). On December 9, 1944 a group of scientists, engineers and German Army & Navy officials met to discuss the "use of the A4 from sea, towed by U-boats." A secret transcript of that discussion went on to state, in effect:

> Dr. Dickmann explained the plan by which the A-4 could be towed by a single submarine, submerged in a waterproof launch container to a favorable firing position off an enemy's coast. From there the device (A-4/V-2) could be fired from the launch platform which would be expended, allowing the submarine to return to home port.

By December of 1944 development of such a project was allegedly begun at Peenemunde's "Prufstand XII" (Test-stand 12), under the direction of engineering officer, Brigadier General (Generalmajor) Josef Rossmann and engineer, Walter (also listed as Walther) J.H. "Papa" Riedel (head of the Peenemunde Design Bureau).

Allegedly code-named "Projekt Schwimmweste" (Project Life-Vest) the sea-launched A-4/V-2 plan was based upon the manufacture of a number of 105 foot (32 meter) long, 300 ton (one source described them as being 98 feet long and 500 tons), towed submersible launch containers, Raketensilos (rocket-silos) or so-called "underwater lighter" barges (referred to by the Germans as "Apparat-F" or "Apparatus-F"), and a contract for at least three such containers designed to launch the A-4/V-2 guided rocket was given to AG Vulcan Werft shipbuilding company (under the direction of a mysterious "Dr. Dickmann") at the Stettin Shipyard in early December of 1944 (the Dickman letter diagrams of Apparatus-F would have made it approximately 120 feet in length). According to Dr. Michael J. Neufeld, Curator of the NASM, however: "Schwimmweste has often been falsely connected to Prufstand XII, but in fact it was a floating test stand for Wasserfall" (an experimental anti-aircraft missile). Because of persistent Allied bombing raids on German shipyards and industrial facilities, however, it is believed that only one of the submersible barge-launchers was constructed before the end of the war in Europe.

Had such rocket-silo barges been deployed before Germany's surrender, the greatly increased hydrodynamic drag associated with the towing of such rocket-silo barges would have resulted in tremendous fuel consumption by the towing U-boats. As a result, they would have required either mid-ocean refueling, or the use of as many as two Type IXC or Type XXI U-boats (planned to have been modified for the task of towing by the shipbuilding firms of Blohm & Voss in Hamburg and AG Weser in Bremen). The U-boats would have taken turns in towing each launch container across the North Atlantic to the American East coast, to have retained sufficient fuel capacity to complete a round trip back to Europe. Another proposed solution to the fuel consumption problem would have been to install additional fuel cells in the silo-barges, from which the mother U-boats would have been refueled. One source indicated that the Type XXI U-boats would have been capable of towing as many as three rocket-silo barges at a time, however the extreme hydrodynamic drag and increased fuel consumption associated with such an arrangement would have made such an operation highly unlikely. There were at the time a few extreme-long-range U-boats, primarily of the Type IXD-2 class, that had sufficient fuel bunkerage to have been able to complete a round-trip, silo-barge tow to the American Northeast coast without the need for refueling, the *U-873* having been one such boat.

The rocket-silo barges were designed to have slight positive buoyancy, only remaining submerged by the forward momentum of the tow. Once at the appropriate launch site, a position South of Nantucket Shoals, approximately 185 miles off the coast of New York City, crewmen would board the barges, attach power and launch command cables from the "mother" U-boats, and flood ballast tanks to invert them perpendicular to the surface. They would then fuel-up the missiles, each with more than 8 tons of ethyl-alcohol and liquid oxygen (as well as hydrogen-peroxide and heated sodium-permanganate to power their 600 horse-power fuel pumps), set the rockets' gyroscopic guidance systems and open the water-tight bow caps for launch. The launch crews would then return to the U-boats from which the remote launch commands would have been carried out.

The rockets' hot combustion "efflux" gasses would have been ducted away from the missiles and vectored up 180 degrees, exiting into the atmosphere from vents at the top, outer edges of the launch silos. Sources conflict regarding the status of the production of the A-4/V-2 "Apparat-F" rocket-silo barges, with some indicating that at least one such barge had been completed at the Schichau dockyard at Elbing before the end of the war in Europe (though it was never located by the invading Allies), while others indicate that the Kriegsmarine had cancelled the order for the barges in late December of 1944. It had been reported by a Markus Korberl, and later published, that the Type VIIC-41 U-boat *U-1063* under command of Kapitanleutnant Karl-Heinz Stephan, took part in at least one sea trial while towing a submersible barge. There is, however, a lack of sufficient official documentation to prove that such a trial actually took place. In any case, there are serious doubts as to whether German technology had advanced sufficiently to have made the project operational by the time of Germany's capitulation.

Additionally, though German military authorities clearly entertained the possibility of attacking a major American Northeast coastal city with submarine launched V-Type weapons, there is no solid evidence that a specific plan was ever mobilized to actually carry out such an attack. German war planners had earlier begun the research toward the development of a super-long-range bomber capable of round-trip bombing raids from Germany to the American Northeast coast, and back. Likewise, Germany's development of the so-called "Amerika-Bomber" (the most likely candidate for such an operational strategic-bomber might have been the four-jet engine, flying-wing type concept prototype, Horten "Ho-18"), which was never completed because the technical challenges posed by the vast distance across the Atlantic Ocean, kept the Third Reich's development of such weapons at bay, before the Axis surrender in Europe.

On April 24, 1945 the Type IXC/40 U-boat, *U-546* under command of Kapitanleutnant Paul Just, torpedoed and sank the Edsall-Class U.S. Navy destroyer escort U.S.S. *Frederick C. Davis* (*DE-136*), Southeast of Cape Farewell, Greenland, with the loss of 126 of her 192 Officers and crewmen. The *Frederick C. Davis* was the last American warship lost to enemy action in the Atlantic theater during the war (the U.S. Navy sub-chaser U.S.S. *Eagle 56* (*PE-56*) had been torpedoed and sunk several hours earlier, on 23 April 1945 by the German U-boat *U-853* under command of Oberleutnant zur See, Helmut Frömsdorf). The *U-546* quickly came under attack by the destroyer escort U.S.S. *Flaherty* (*DE-135*), was depth-charged to the surface and sunk with the loss of 24 of her Officers and crewmen. Commander Just and 32 Officers and crewmen were rescued by the U.S.S. *Flaherty* and other Allied warships, and were landed at Argentia, Newfoundland. Commander Just, 2 Officers and 5 technical specialists from the *U-546* were placed in solitary confinement and subjected to daily beatings and torture by U.S. Naval intelligence personnel, as they were brutally interrogated about the suspected rocket launching U-boats. According to one highly credible U.S. Navy historical source, once hustled to the Navy brig (jail):

> Just was subjected to what has to be described as "shock interrogation," preceeded [*sic*] by exhaustive physical exercise and beatings, treatment also inflicted on his seven shipmates.

They were later transferred to Washington, D.C. where the beatings and interrogations continued until May 9, 1945, when Commander Just agreed to cooperate with his captors. This was believed to have been the same interrogation team that later "debriefed" Commander Steinhoff and several of his Officers and crewmen.

A number of secret Office of Strategic Services "OSS" (the forerunner of the CIA) reports from Stockholm, Sweden, warned American authorities as early as October of 1944 of a suspected concerted U-boat missile attack against New York City, and on December 10, 1944 New York's Mayor Fiorello LaGuardia caused a near panic when he mentioned to the press the possibility of such an attack. In early January of 1945 Germany's Chief of War Production, Albert Speer, boasted in a Berlin Radio propaganda broadcast that V-Type weapons "would fall on New York by February 1st 1945." According to a formerly Top Secret "Ultra" report from the U.S. Navy's radio signal decryption unit known as "Op-20-G": "Reliable agents reported observing U/B's (U-boats) in Norway that looked as if V-rails ("vengeance weapon" launch rails) were being laid on deck." On January 8, 1945 Admiral Jonas Ingram, who had relieved Admiral Ingersoll as CINCLANT (Commander in Chief of the U.S. Navy's Atlantic Fleet), believing the American people had become too complacent, also raised public fear by announcing the possibility of a U-boat launched missile attack against the American

Northeast coast. Admiral Ingram, however, attempted to quell the sensation he had created, revealing that the U.S. Navy's Tenth Fleet had been mobilized to thwart just such an attack. Based upon that information and the interrogations of numerous captured German U-boat Officers, crewmen and Abwehr agents, intercepted and decrypted "Enigma" radio transmissions, and the knowledge that ten U-boats including six U-boats comprising Seewolf group, had recently departed their Norwegian bases headed on some unknown mission to the American East coast, the U.S. Navy mobilized "Operation Teardrop."

Teardrop (initially code-named "Bumblebee") was an aggressive anti-submarine campaign intended to intercept and destroy the suspected rocket-launching U-boats before they could reach their respective launch positions off the American Northeast coast. The massive U.S. Navy Tenth Fleet armada was comprised of four escort carrier hunter/killer task force groups including more than forty destroyers (DDs) and destroyer escorts (DEs), formed in two successive barriers. The U.S. Navy escort "jeep" carriers included the Casablanca-class U.S.S. *Mission Bay* (*CVE-59*) and the Bogue-Class U.S.S. *Croatan* (*CVE-25*) assisted by twenty escorts covering the Northern Atlantic approaches, as well as the U.S.S. *Bogue* (*CVE-9*) and the *Bogue*-Class carrier U.S.S. *Core* (*CVE-13*), assisted by twenty-two escorts, to the South. Four of the suspect U-boats (all Seewolf group boats that were not exercising strict radio discipline), including the Type IXC *U-518* (Oberleutnant zur See [Lieutenant, senior grade] Hans Offerman); and the IXC/40 Types *U-546* (KL Paul Just), *U-880* (KL Gerhard Schotzau), and *U-1235* (KL Franz Barsch), were located by Allied naval and air forces (primarily through detection by high-frequency direction-finding, or HF/DF radio signal transmission intercepts) and destroyed while transiting the North Atlantic, though six boats made it to their respective patrol areas before Germany surrendered. Only Seewolf group boats *U-805* and *U-858* survived to surrender to U.S. Naval forces.

On April 29, 1945 Adolf Hitler married Eva Braun in a private ceremony in his Berlin bunker (Führerbunker), and he appointed Kriegsmarine Grossadmiral, Karl Dönitz, as his chosen successor, as the second and last Führer (Leader). On April 30, 1945 Hitler and his bride committed suicide, and Dönitz assumed leadership of the Third Reich. On May 4, 1945 at 3:14 PM (GMT), the German High Command began transmitting a repeated radio dispatch from "BdU" (Befehlshaber der Unterseeboote) "Commander in Chief, U-boats' Grossadmiral Donitz, ordering: "All U-boats, attention all U-boats, cease fire at once, stop all hostile action against Allied shipping, Dönitz."

Back to The *U-873*

Kapitanleutnant Steinhoff, commanding the *U-873* and headed into the North Atlantic on her way to hunt shipping in the Caribbean, received the German High Command radio dispatch, but rather than surrender to British or Canadian forces, Commander Steinhoff continued on his original course. After snorkeling from Norway into the North Atlantic and remaining submerged for 15 straight days, the *U-873* set course for the American Northeast coast. By May 5th she proceeded submerged, snorkeling by days and surfaced at night in order to receive signals from BdU. On May 6th they were instructed to obey only coded signals from BdU, and on the 7th a signal was received ordering them to return to Norway, though just a few hours later they received news of Germany's unconditional surrender to the Allies. Disobeying BdU's orders to return to Norway, the *U-873* dove to 180 meters and proceeded on a Southerly course. A number of her Officers attempted to persuade Commander Steinhoff to "sail to South America and there attempting to sell the items stored in the (*U-873*'s) keel duct" to buy safe passage to Argentina, but relenting to objections by his crew, Steinhoff decided to surrender to the United States.

In a converted munitions warehouse at the Washington (D.C.) Navy Yard, 41-year-old Commander Kenneth A. Knowles, head of the U.S. Navy's top-secret "Ultra" Decryption Center and Submarine-

Tracking Room (part of the Communications Security Section of the Office of Naval Communications) known as "Op20G" (Op-20-G), gave daily briefings to top Navy brass regarding the movements of German U-boats in the North Atlantic. Constantly monitoring German encrypted radio transmissions employing their newest four-rotor "Enigma" code referred to as "Triton" ("Shark" to the British), Op-20-G had been tracking the enemy's U-boat operations for much of the war. First to a liaison to the Commander-in-Chief of the U.S. Navy (COMINCH), then to the C-in-C of the Atlantic Fleet (CINCLANT), the daily enemy sub position estimates were sent down the chain of command to local naval authorities, alerting them to the possible presence of German U-boats in their respective areas of operation. With particular scrutiny given to the boats of Seewolf group, elements of Operation Teardrop were directed to positions most likely to intercept with the courses of the approaching U-boat threat.

On May 8, 1945 the war with Germany was officially over (though some German forces on the Eastern Front held out until the 11th), and on May 9th the U-*873* received a radio signal from BdU ordering her "to report their position and in accordance with this position, proceed to a designated Allied harbor." On the morning of May 11th "the engineering officer Leitender Ingenieur (LI) Chief Engineer, Oberleutnant (Lieutenant, senior grade) Helmut Jurgens, gave the order to set course for the nearest American port." About an hour later the *U-873* detected a radar contact on her Tunis radar detector set, prompting her to submerge. "Sometime later, and after hydrophone contacts from several different directions were received, *U-873* surfaced and reported her position." The *U-873* was directed by a U.S. Navy radio transmission to surface, switch on her navigation lights, to fly a black (not white) surrender flag (for increased visibility on the horizon) from her periscope (as per order of Royal Navy Admiral, Sir Harold M. Burrough, acting for General Eisenhower), to disarm all torpedoes, jettison all gun ammunition and secure all guns facing aft. Though obeying, Steinhoff and other surrendering U-boat commanders took the order to fly a black flag as an insult, being the symbol of piracy. After surfacing, the *U-873* crew jettisoned her boat's log-book, secret documents and sensitive equipment including all of her Type V (T-5) passive-acoustic-homing torpedoes, Enigma radio signal encryption/decryption machine, Kurier (courier) radio burst-transmitter, Tunis radar-detector, classified equipment manuals, charts and code-books, and displayed the black surrender flag, as ordered. The "*U-873* then proceeded in accordance with instructions received by signal and was met by the U.S.S. *Vance*."

The Surrender

In the early morning hours of Tuesday, May 11, 1945, while escorting a merchant convoy to the Mediterranean, in the area Northwest of the Azores the U.S. Coast Guard manned Edsall Class destroyer escorts U.S.S. *Vance* (*DE-387*) and U.S.S. *Durant* (*DE-389*) spotted a light in the distance. Having received orders to keep a lookout for the surrendering *U-873*, the *Vance* and *Durant* closed on the light, which the *Durant* illuminated with her 24 inch spotlight, revealing the surfaced U-boat. The *Durant* hailed the "erstwhile enemy" over her public address system, established the *U-873*'s identity and ordered her to heave-to for boarding. The *Vance* placed a 21 man prize crew aboard the *U-873* (under U.S. Navy Commander Christopher C. Knapp), and broke off from the convoy to escort her as ordered to the American Northeast coast, where she arrived off the Portsmouth, New Hampshire Navy Base on Sunday the 16th of May. The *U-873* was temporarily anchored off the Kitt's Rock Buoy located approximately a mile out from the Whaleback Lighthouse at the entrance of Portsmouth harbor, where U.S. Navy demolition experts checked the submarine for booby-traps and allegedly secured her scuttling-charges and other explosive ordnance.

The U-*873* was taken over by the Naval Surrender Group under command of U.S. Navy Commander Thomas K. Kimmel (listed by one source as J. Kincair, but more probably "Kinkaid" Kimmell), and was escorted into the Portsmouth Navy Base by the U.S.S. *Vance,* in the early afternoon of the 17th. According to the surface group Commander of the U.S. Navy's Eastern Sea Frontier's Northern Group, Captain Alexander W. Moffat, Commander

> Steinhoff was a tough, truculent Nazi.[6] When he came aboard (U.S. Coast Guard Cutter) *Argo* (*CGC-100*) he refused to talk to me. Through an interpreter he said only: "I am obeying orders of a higher authority." Then he sneered at me and turned away.

In subsequent interrogations of the *U-873*'s crew, it appears that Commander Steinhoff may have been suffering from the stress of his command in those trying times, and may have been losing control of his boat prior to his surrender.

> He was described by his crew as an excellent seaman but totally unable to exercise his command. The engineer officer (LI, Helmut Jurgens, then 25 years of age) and the doctor (Dr. Karl Wilhelm Reinke, then 28) aboard the *U-873* seemed to have influenced the Commanding Officer to such an extent that they were, for all particular purposes, in command of the boat.

A number of other German U-boats also surrendered at the Portsmouth, New Hampshire Navy Base that week, including the Type IXC/40 boats *U-1228* under Oberleutnant zur See Friedrich-Wilhelm Marinfeld on May 13th; the *U-805* under Korvettenkapitan Richard Bernardelli and the *U-858* under Kapitanleutnant Thilo Bode on May 14th; and the Type XB *U-234* under KL Johann-Heinrich Fehler, allegedly on May 19th (All of the German U-boats that surrendered to U.S. Naval forces were received at Portsmouth, New Hampshire, some of which were later towed to ports along the American Northeast coast on so-called "Victory Visits").

Once disembarked at the Portsmouth Navy Base pier,

Commander Steinhoff was photographed by the local press, and "announced (through an interpreter) that he would give a press conference soon." Two German Officers and 5 crewmen remained under U.S. Marine guard aboard the U-*873* as Commander Steinhoff and 52 of his Officers and crewmen were turned over to First Naval District officials at the Portsmouth (NH) Naval Prison (referred to as "The Rock" and "The Castle"), the Portsmouth Naval Prison is actually located on Seavey Island in Kittery, Maine, across the Piscataqua River from Portsmouth, New Hampshire), where they were photographed, fingerprinted and interviewed. During his initial interview by U.S. Naval authorities "it was determined that Fritz (*sic*) Steinhoff, skipper of the *U-873* was suffering from a heart condition." Commander Kimmell erroneously reported to the press that "the *U-873* had fired on a tanker while in waters off Norway within the last two weeks. Six of the ship's 15 torpedoes were missing at the time of capture." In fact, however, no such attack was made against Allied shipping by the *U-873* on her one and only combat patrol, and the alleged "missing" torpedoes actually had been the advanced passive-acoustic-homing (of which she had actually only been carrying five) T-5s, which were intentionally jettisoned by her crew as ordered, in preparation for her surrender.

Unknown to Commander Steinhoff, back in Germany his brother Ernst, General Dornberger, Dr. von Braun and many other top German rocket scientists had surrendered to American Army forces and were undergoing extensive interrogations by Allied intelligence agents (including members of the "United States Naval Technical Mission in Europe"), about their work on guided rockets. Between May 16th and 18th 1945 Dr. Steinhoff (repeatedly erroneously listed as Dr. Steinho[**t**] in the Navy's Technical Mission Report), was interrogated by a Dr. E.H. Krause and F/L H.R. Brock, about such subjects as radar beam missile guidance, rocket-efflux (jet-stream) ionization, homing systems and proximity fuses, among other highly technical weapons related matters. Likewise, Dr. Steinhoff knew nothing about his brother Friedrich's surrender to U.S. Naval forces in the North Atlantic, nor of the strange circumstances surrounding his subsequent, quick and mysterious demise.

While the surrendered U-boats were interned at the Portsmouth Navy Base, U.S. Navy and Marine personnel took part in what can only be described as an undisciplined, free-for-all, including drinking, sleeping while on watch and the looting of virtually everything of value from the boats, and their Officers and crewmen. According to one U.S. Naval Intelligence report . . .

> All four boats carried large quantities of liquor. Up to 21 May only *U-805* had been completely stripped of movable gear. According to the Captain of *U-234*, this boat originally carried approximately 900 bottles of liquor (actually mostly liter bottles of Beck's beer, rather than hard liquor). Only a part of this liquor has been located to date and removed from the ship. On the morning of 20 May, Lt. Ewald of Op-20-G boarded *U-234* and found U.S. Naval ratings drunk aboard. At various times on 20 and 21 May U.S. Naval ratings were found asleep in the bunks while on duty in *U-234*. There has been a certain amount of drinking by U.S.N. personnel aboard *U-873* and *U-1228*, but no where to the extent that it took place on *U-234*."

At the time of her surrender, the *U-234* had been headed for Japan and was carrying strategic cargo including, among other war related materials, 560 kilograms (approximately 1,200 lbs.) of 77.7% pure uranium-oxide (though not quite the enriched, weapon grade isotope U235), destined for use in the Japanese atomic research program.

From recently declassified handwritten U.S. Naval Prison notes taken during the initial interrogation of *U-873* Officers and crewmen while held in the Portsmouth Naval Prison, it is clear the interrogators also learned that Commander Steinhoff had previously been the Commanding Officer of "*U-511* as C.O. on first patrol June 42" during which Germany's first successful submarine rocket-firing tests were conducted. Steinhoff's first brutal two and a half hour long interrogation took place in an isolated dungeon-like cell known by the prison's Marine guards as "The Pit." Upon discovery of Steinhoff's involvement in the secret research and testing of submarine launched rockets, and his insistence that no such U-boats were ever deployed, it is likely that Steinhoff's interrogations, while "lashed to a wooden chair" grew increasingly more brutal. Nearly six decades after the incident, in June of 2003 retired U.S. Navy Captain Jerry Mason interviewed the *U-873*'s former Oberfunkmaat (Radioman 2nd Class), Georg Seitz, who recalled that:

> He [Seitz] saw Steinhoff returning to his cell after his initial interrogation with his [Steinhoff's] face swollen and bloody which confirms that his interrogation was more brutal than portrayed in the Inspector General's report.

Commander Steinhoff, two Officers and 47 crewmen were transferred in several heavily guarded Navy buses later that day to Boston, Massachusetts, where they were handed over to the First Army Command authorities and temporarily held at the Suffolk County Jail on Charles Street. According to Captain Moffat:

> The Hotel Thorndike in Boston had been taken over by the Army (note: Captain Moffat may have actually been referring to the Hotel "Buckminster"), as a clearinghouse for all prisoners of war arriving in Boston for further disposition to prisoner of war camps in the South. A shipload of prisoners had just arrived from overseas, so the Hotel was full to capacity. Therefore, the crew of *U-873* was housed in the Charles Street Jail in Boston.

They were to be held in Boston until transfer to PoW camps at Fort Hunt in Alexandria, Virginia, Fort George G. Meade in

Maryland, and Camp McCain in Mississippi, on May 19th.

Even though the war with Germany had been over for more than a week, a number of U-boats were still unaccounted for. At least one such boat remained at sea until August 17, 1945, more than three months after Germany's capitulation, when the Type VIIC, *U-977* under command of Oberleutnant zur See, Heinz Schaffer, surrendered at Mar del Plata, Argentina.[7] At the time of his interrogations, Commander Steinhoff had been out-of-the-loop of the submarine launched rocket research program for more than two years, and aside from scant information he might have received from his brother Ernst, he may have known little or nothing about the A-4/V-2 rocket-silo barge ("Apparatus-F") project.

Before the end of World War II the U.S. Navy's Gato Class submarine U.S.S. *Barb* (*SS-220*) under Commander Eugene B. Fluckey, also took part in rocket attacks against the enemy. During the *Barb*'s 12th and last war patrol, on the evening of July 25, 1945, she surfaced off the East coast of Karafuto Island and fired thirty-two 5-inch rockets into the factory town of Shiritory, followed later that evening by a 12 rocket attack on the coastal town of Kashiho, causing panic among the Japanese populace. There is no evidence that the *Barb* attacks were inspired by the German experiments, but rather appear to have been inspired by Commander Fluckey and naval ordnance personnel who jerry-rigged Mk-51 launch tubes (like those fitted aboard U.S. Navy & Marine amphibious assault landing craft) to the *Barb*'s deck, from which standard U.S. Navy "High Velocity Spin-stabilized Rockets" (HVSRs) were fired. Twelve such launch tubes were fitted to the deck of the *Barb*, which could be electrically fired in salvo in just 4.5 seconds. With a range of only a few thousand yards, their small 9.6 pound warheads did more to disturb enemy morale, than actual tactical or strategic destruction of the Japanese war-making infrastructure. Unlike the rocket test firings from the *U-511*, however, the *Barb*'s rockets could only be launched while the submarine was surfaced.

The Mysterious Death of Commander Steinhoff

During the evening of May 18, 1945, it is believed the U.S. Naval Intelligence "debriefing team" returned to Commander Steinhoff's "squalid cell," where they resumed their brutal interrogation regarding the suspected secret rocket/missile launching U-boats. Kapitanleutnant Johann-Heinrich Fehler, Commander of the surrendered *U-234*, who had been held in the cell adjacent to Commander Steinhoff, later recounted how he was unable to sleep that night due to the agonizing sounds of his comrade's torture. According to a letter typed by Commander Fehler, forty (40) years after his experiences under U.S. military custody in New England:

> . . . in the very night, when the crew of *U 234* had been locked up in the Boston county jail, on her way from Portsmouth (Mass) (actually New Hampshire) to Camp "Fort G. Meade" (Fort George G. Meade in Maryland), the crew of another German submarine was herded into this jail and locked up on the same floor of the same wing of this jail. A solid brickwall separated the two crews only. The captain of this boat was Kapitanleutnant Steinhoff. He was locked up in the same cell on the other side of the brickwall corresponding to my own cell. During this only

> night in the Boston-county-jail sleep was impossible for me. From the neighborhood I heard continuous shouting, moaning and sounds of beating. I could not understand anything. But the noises kept me awake until the early morning hours. When this other crew was herded downstairs the next morning I noticed some uproar in front of the cell opposite to my own. But I could not make out any reason for it. It was only two or three weeks later, when I met the ships doctor of the other submarine, a certain Marinestabsartz Dr. Brehme (actually Dr. Reinke), who told me that he had tried to save Steinhoff who had slashed his wrist and had lost a large amount of blood. It took several hours until infusion liquid was delivered and that in a large city like Boston. So Steinhoff died although he easeky (*sic*: easily) could have been saved.[8]

Steinhoff's interrogators were a covert team from the Office of Naval Intelligence (ONI) "Special Activities Branch" code-named "Op-16-Z" (also allegedly known as "Z-Group"), out of Fort Hunt, and was headed by an over-zealous civilian "Chief Interrogator" by the name of Jack Henry Alberti. Apparently, Alberti was known to dress in the uniform of a U.S. Navy Lieutenant Commander, and is believed to have identified himself to his captives under interrogation, by the alias of "Lieutenant Commander Alvares" as he had been known to Commander Fehler.

According to U.S. Naval Intelligence authorities, Steinhoff was "broken down" by the "interrogation," however, they went on to add: "the only violence that was used was being slapped in the face by one of our enlisted men when he was slow to answer questions." Another U.S. Navy account claimed that his interrogators "may have slapped his face once to snap him out of a deep depression." At 8:00 AM on May 19, 1945, more than a week after the war with Germany had ended, Commander Steinhoff was allegedly discovered in his cell on

Tier 5 of the Charles Street Jail (one source indicates the discovery was made at 4:00 AM), lying in a pool of blood. *U-873*'s physician, Dr. Karl Wilhelm Reinke, was advised of Commander Steinhoff's condition, and he demanded that Steinhoff immediately be given a blood transfusion or plasma. After a two and a half hour delay in delivering plasma to Commander Steinhoff, however, Dr. Reinke realized his captors were "not interested in keeping [Steinhoff] alive." Commander Steinhoff was transported to the Massachusetts General Hospital where he was pronounced dead at 10:00 AM. The Massachusetts General Hospital's emergency room in the then, newly built George Robert White Memorial Building was less than 200 yards from the Charles Street Jail. The Boston Medical Examiner, assisted by a U.S. Army physician, Colonel Keeley, determined the cause of death was "suicide" later that morning. Mrs. Rita (Rand) Conroy, then a nurse receptionist at the Massachusetts General Hospital emergency room later recounted a heated exchange between hospital staff, and a U.S. Navy Officer accompanied by a Marine guard (almost certainly "Jack" Alberti and Marine PFC Sol Levanthal), as the Navy Officer demanded the immediate handing over of Steinhoff's body to his custody. The Navy Officer threatened that if he was forced to do so, he would "carry away the corpse slung over his shoulder, but that he was not leaving the hospital without Steinhoff's body."

According to a May 21, 1945 letter from Colonel A. J. Lamoreux, Chief, Provost Marshal Branch (H.Q. 1st Service Command) Security and Intelligence Division of the U.S. Army, to the Provost Marshal General (subject: Transfer of German Navy Prisoners of War, *U-873*):

> German Navy Prisoner of War Officer, Kapitan-leutnant Steinhoff, Fritz (actually Friedrich), internment #1G-445NA, committed suicide on 19 May 1945 by severing an artery in his wrist with a broken piece of eyeglass and a wire which apparently came from his cap.

One physical prerequisite for any World War II German U-boat Commander was perfect 20/20 vision, and Commander Steinhoff was not known by his family nor by his fellow Officers or crewmen, to wear glasses. Several other versions regarding the circumstances surrounding Commander Steinhoff's mysterious death were later circulated by U.S. Navy sources, one indicating that he

> used the heel of his shoe to bend open a wire hook on the spring of his cot. With this he had raked open his wrist and bled to death, found by a guard making morning rounds.

Another source indicated that Commander Steinhoff severed an artery in his wrist with a "piece of the broken crystal from his wristwatch." Though another account claimed the broken glass he allegedly used to sever an artery in his wrist came from a pair of "sunglasses," but it is highly unlikely that Commander Steinhoff would have been allowed to retain either sunglasses or a wristwatch while in confinement. Official U.S. military protocol (pursuant to CNO and CominCh directive: (e) of the "Procedure for Handling Prisoners of War"), instructed that:

> **EVERYTHING MUST BE TAKEN FROM THE PRISONERS except necessary clothing.**

Furthermore, a subsequent investigation revealed that personal effects such as watches, medals and decorations, Officer's caps, Leica and Bessa cameras, navigational and dental/surgical instruments, helmet(s), ceremonial dagger(s) and a bottle of brandy had been looted from the prisoners by the Navy and Marine guards, and a civilian Industrial Manager at the Portsmouth Naval Base later testified that he "observed many bulging pockets" among the U.S. military personnel leaving the *U-873*. At one point, a U.S. Marine Warrant Officer named McGraw said to Jack Alberti, "some of the prisoners are complaining about their watches being taken," to which Alberti responded, "To hell with it, don't pay any attention to it!" In a report on 22 May 1945, Jack Alberti made the obvious attempt at distancing himself from those dishonorable activities, reporting that :

> . . . all items of value, such as watches, rings, decorations, wallets, even those containing personal photographs, etc. were looted from the prisoners. In some instances where enlisted men had taken watches from prisoners, these watches were taken from the enlisted men by Marine officers who retained them as souvenirs.

In a belated attempt to curtail such activities, the military authorities decided to make an example of U.S. Navy and Marine personnel taking part in such conduct, and at least one unfortunate Navy enlisted man paid a high price for what might otherwise have been viewed as a minor indiscretion. According to Alberti's report:

> On 21 May the Marine guard on *U-234* reported finding a pack of German playing cards on one of the naval working parties leaving *U-234*. Admiral Withers, Commandant of the Portsmouth Navy Yard, has ordered a deck court martial for this man.

With the many inconsistent stories regarding the mysterious circumstances surrounding his death, it may never be known for certain whether Commander Steinhoff died at the hands of his interrogators, or whether he actually committed suicide, possibly in a state of depression, hoping to avoid further beatings at the hands of his captors. Medical experts have given their opinion that contrary to common belief, it would have been extremely difficult for Steinhoff to have cut the radial artery in his wrist in the manner alleged:

> without extensive knowledge of anatomy (and a surgical quality cutting instrument such as a scalpel). Most of the

attempts are without success because of the very well sheltered position of that artery and its characteristic that this vessel can contract and stop bleeding if not completely cut through.

A prominent Medical Examiner reviewed the circumstances surrounding the alleged suicide of Commander Steinhoff, and came to the following conclusion:

> I can not conceive that even the most psychotic individual could actually damage the Radial Artery in the way described. In my experience even suicidal persons armed with razor blades never did more than wipe out a nerve or two and sever tendons.

On the 60th anniversary of Commander Steinhoff's death, in 2005 U.S. Army Reserve Colonel Frank E. Wismer, III, a Chaplain with the 94th Regional Readiness Command stationed at Fort Devens, who has researched the Steinhoff case, raised some interesting questions regarding his alleged suicide. According to Colonel Wismer:

> Steinhoff said that he would be making a statement to the press . . . Generally, people who commit suicide don't do it if they've made some sort of commitment. Of course, if he'd been beaten and had an interview pending with the press, that would not look good for Alberti and company.
>
> Colonel Wismer added that "It appears abundantly clear to me that he was killed (murdered) while under interrogation. I also found it noteworthy that Sol Leventhal, a Jew, would be the individual chosen to help with the "interview" of a Nazi. Finally, I came across his [Steinhoff's] death certificate. I noticed on the certificate that there is something that has been Xed out by typewriter.

> I have been curious to learn what that **it** [*sic*] and wonder if it suggests something other than suicide.

Colonel Wismer was correct, that a line under the "Cause and Manner" (of death), listed under the words "Incision wound right wrist" has obviously been redacted from the official record, and only close forensic examination of the original document might shed light on the "deleted" cause. The fact that the Death Certificate indicates that the incision was on the "right wrist" raises even more questions, particularly since Commander Steinhoff was clearly "right handed." Several physicians and a forensic pathologist were asked about that discrepancy, and they all agreed that a suicidal individual would have used his dominant (strong) hand to lacerate the subordinate (weak) extremity. The alleged facts purporting to prove that Commander Steinhoff committed suicide therefore, raise more doubts than they do to support the suspect suicide conclusion.

The suicide theory also remains difficult to believe because Steinhoff knew that the war was then over, and he must have realized that it was only a matter of time before he and his crew would be returned to Germany for repatriation, where he would once again be reunited with his beloved wife and children. The Commanders of the U-boats that surrendered at Portsmouth, New Hampshire, chose to surrender to American forces believing they would receive fair treatment under the Geneva Convention protocols. They also knew that their internment as prisoners of war would only be a temporary setback, and that before long they would be returned to Germany to be reunited with their families. According to U.S. Navy Captain Alexander W. Moffat, German U-boat Commander Johann-Heinrich Fehler of the *U-234*, told him

> in perfect English with a suggestion of Oxford accent . . . "In a few years you will see Germany reborn. In the meantime, I shall have a welcome rest at one of your prisoner of war camps with better food, I am sure, than I

> have had in months. Then I'll be repatriated ready to work for a new economic empire."

For most of the surrendered U-boat men, the future was not bleak. For them, the war was over, and their situations could only get better with time. Why then, would Commander Steinhoff have committed suicide? Would Commander Steinhoff, a devoted and honorable father and husband, actually have committed suicide, knowing that his wife was about to give birth to their third child? Commander Steinhoff's wife, Ilse, back home in the ravages of post-war Germany, gave birth to their third son, Joern, just ten (10) days after her husband's death, not yet knowing of his mysterious and tragic fate. Commander Steinhoff was simply a tragic victim of unique historical circumstances . . . truly an example of "the wrong man, finding himself in the wrong place, at the wrong time."

In June of 1945 the Inspector General of the U.S. Navy conducted an investigation into: "Irregularities conducted with the handling of surrendered German submarines and prisoners of war at the Navy Yard, Portsmouth, New Hampshire." According to the investigation, Jack Alberti, though a civilian, conducted his interrogations of the German PoWs while "wearing the uniform of a Lieutenant Commander of the (U.S.) Navy." Alberti claimed to have been given "special authority of the Director of Naval Intelligence" (allegedly by Captain John L. Riheldaffer), to wear the Lieutenant Commander's uniform and to "assign and distribute (loot) souvenirs collected from submarines that had no intelligence value," though the investigation report went on to state that "He has no written authority for doing so."

According to the investigation report, Alberti testified to the effect:

> Lieutenant Commander Steinhoff, Commanding Officer of *U-873*, was a very difficult prisoner—adamant. Steinhoff was the only person who could supply certain

information considered of prime importance (almost certainly about the suspected rocket launching U-boats), so he [Alberti] requested the Commandant of the prison (U.S. Marine Colonel Joseph A. Rossell) to assign him a large, husky Marine, to stand by while he interrogated Steinhoff. He directed that Marine (Private First Class, Sol Leventhal) to stand outside the door. He interrogated Steinhoff two and one-half hours. It was a tough battle. He instructed the Marine that if he gave the nod, to give the prisoner one slap with the back of his hand. That was done. The slap in the face he was given was not hard enough to be called real physical violence. It was used for insulting purposes, but resulted in Steinhoff's breaking down and giving the information that was needed.

The investigation report went on to say:

Private First Class Sol Leventhal stated, in effect, in sworn testimony that he was a member of the special group of guards who were selected for the handling of prisoners who might appear to be difficult. Those men were picked to do what they were told and keep quiet. Captain Steinhoff went in the room with Mr. Alberti, and he (Leventhal) was called in. Steinhoff was being questioned as to the movements of his submarine. Alberti indicated to him that he was to slap Steinhoff, which he did, two smart slaps—one with the palm, the other with the back of his hand. They were not resisted. Steinhoff then gave the desired information. (He later committed suicide in Boston.)

Clearly, however, this alleged "tough truculent Nazi" would not have been "broken down" by a few mere slaps in the face, and the evidence indicates that Commander Steinhoff suffered a far more vigorous physical interrogation. Steinhoff, an alleged (but unconfirmed) National Socialist "True Believer" (though not a member of the Nazi party), refused to cooperate with his interrogators, and his stalwart recalcitrance may have contributed to his brutal treatment. Furthermore, Steinhoff may have been considered to be "expendable" by his interrogators (and by high ranking officials in the Office of Naval Intelligence), possibly fearing post-war (Cold War) international scrutiny, should the story of his tortuous interrogation, in clear violation of the Articles of the Geneva Convention, later come to public light. Nowhere in the disclosed official records is Jack Alberti's presence accounted for at the Portsmouth, New Hampshire Navy Base between May 18th and 19th of 1945, and even 60 years ago it was merely a 3 hour trip between Portsmouth and Boston, by either train or automobile.

The U.S. Navy's investigation into Op-16-Z's conduct in the interrogation of the surrendered German U-boat Officers and crewmen went to great lengths to justify Jack Alberti's unlawful techniques, by including in their report the following specious explanation:

> He (Alberti) stated he was familiar years ago with the provisions of the Geneva Convention, that he understood they were not to follow in detail the provisions of that in that the prisoners were not yet prisoners of war in so far as they at the Prison were concerned, since they were simply detaining them until arrangements could be made to take them to Boston where they could come within the full rights of the Geneva Convention. The sole function of the Prison was to hold those fellows until the Naval Intelligence Officers could process them and get them off their hands.

Clearly, however, Alberti's alleged familiarity with the Geneva Conventions, "years ago" was not quite in keeping with the true nature and intent of the Geneva and Hague Convention protocols. Under international law, belligerent combatants could expect to be treated by their enemy captors, with the protections afforded by the Geneva Convention, as soon as their capture or surrender had taken place. Alberti's twisted misinterpretation of the Geneva Convention protocols grew even less credible considering the fact that his initial interrogations were conducted in a military prison (the Portsmouth Naval Prison), rather than the civilian prison (the Charles Street Jail in Boston), where the PoWs were simply held over-night before being transferred to more permanent PoW camps in the South.

Jack Alberti was later involved in another strange incident involving the *U-873*, when . . .

> On the evening of 20 May, at approximately 2330, Mr. Alberti went to the forward part of the conning tower of *U-873* in order to use the telephone which was placed there. In the semi-darkness he stumbled on two boxes. On examination these boxes were found to contain scuttling charges and pull-igniters for same. Mr. Alberti notified Lt. Cdr. Knerr and these charges were removed from the ship. It was not possible to establish who had placed these boxes on the upper deck.

Such dangerous ordnance devices should have been secured and removed from the boat three days earlier, and only by an act of gross negligence or by complete breakdown of discipline and order, could they have been allowed to remain aboard the boat.

In a "Memorandum for Vice Chief of Naval Operations" regarding the report of irregularities with the handling of German prisoners of war at the Portsmouth, New Hampshire Navy Yard, the following findings were presented:

> (a) Serious irregularities reported in the handling of German Prisoners at the Navy Yard, Portsmouth,

were in part caused by the flagrant disregard, by the representatives of Op-16-Z Section of ONI, of the provisions of the Chief Naval Operations' directive of 19 May 1942, serial 01227316, which is in conformity with the Geneva Convention.

(b) Mr. Jack Alberti, a civilian interrogator, wearing a naval uniform while performing the duty of an interrogator greatly exceeded his authority and foundations, when he practically assumed full charge of the examination and processing of prisoners of war at the naval prison. Mr. Alberti had prisoners' decorations removed, distributed looted decorations and personal public property to prison personnel as he saw fit, and caused the commanding officer of a surrendered U-Boat to be slapped by an enlisted man.

(c) Mr. Alberti's actions are in direct violation of the Geneva Convention and the Chief of Naval Operations' directives, and as far as the enemy is aware, he is an American naval officer and his acts were concurred in by the naval command.

As the result of the Navy's investigation and findings, a number of Navy and Marine Officers and enlisted men were subjected to "administrative and disciplinary action," and some court-martialed (for the looting of German PoWs' personal effects), though as a civilian, Jack Alberti evaded any disciplinary actions or prosecution for his misdeeds, by the military authorities. Among those disciplined was U.S. Marine Colonel Joseph A. Rossell, the Commanding Officer of the U.S. Naval Prison at Portsmouth, whose "complete lack of appreciation for his command responsibilities . . . and evidence of complete failure of discipline in the prison . . . [was] considered most reprehensible." A number of distinguished military careers were tarnished, if not destroyed, and possibly at least one life lost due to the much more reprehensible actions of Jack Alberti. Other high ranking U.S. military Officers who were recommended (by Admiral Ernest J. King, the Chief of Naval Personnel and the Commandant, U.S. Marine Corps) to receive "administrative or disciplinary action" because of those events, included: Rear Admiral Withers, Commandant; Captain Clifford H. Roper, Captain of the Portland Navy Yard; Captain Hines (MC) USN, Senior Medical Officer of the Yard; Lt. Comdr. Bromberg (MC) USNR; Major J.P. Mehrlust, USMCR; and Lt. Comdr. S.R. Hatton, USNR (Office of Naval Intelligence).

It is highly likely that the U.S. Navy's Office of Naval Intelligence intentionally chose a civilian like Alberti to lead the "interrogations" so as to allow for unauthorized, unorthodox and unlawful techniques that could not otherwise be sanctioned by the naval authorities. The rather sanitized and self-serving findings of the Navy's so-called "investigation into the irregularities involving the handling of prisoners of war" was further a way of exonerating the Navy of complicity in abrogating the Geneva Convention protocols, for the purpose of extracting information genuinely believed to have been vital to United States national security interests.

The Enigma of Jack Henry Alberti

Jack Henry Alberti was somewhat of a mysterious individual, with a rather strange background for a naval intelligence employee, though official Navy personnel records shed some light on his personal background. Born in Antwerp, Belgium, on March 3, 1902 to Sidney S. Alberti (a naturalized U.S. citizen since 1900), and Maud Elain Speirs, he had allegedly been educated in Belgium, England and Switzerland in history, mathematics, languages and engineering. In 1942 Alberti, a Roman Catholic, was married to forty-year-old Jeanne Waterman, and they resided at 230 Beverly Road, Mt. Lebanon, Pittsburgh, Pennsylvania. Alberti claimed to have been a world traveler, fluent in several languages, including German, and had been employed in numerous capacities, as an assistant civil engineer, as an interior decorator, as a concert pianist, and in the international fruit trade.

Claiming to have had a number of diplomatic contacts, Alberti fled Europe at the outbreak of World War II, and in 1942, at the age of forty-two, he sough employment with the United States Navy's Office of Naval Intelligence, in order "to serve in the capacity for which I am best fitted." After initial doubts about the suitability of his physical condition, the Navy hired him as a probationary "Analyst" at a starting salary of $3,000.00 annually. Alberti quickly rose through the ranks, and salary, receiving a raise to $3,960.00 in October

1942, and became an "Agent under contract" at $4,500.00 annually in July of 1943. In September of 1945 Alberti had been raised to a pay rate equivalent to that of a Lieutenant Commander in the U.S. Navy Reserve, then working under Op-16-PT making $5,026.50, and ultimately to $5,600.00 annually by November of 1945. Based upon official records regarding Jack Alberti, his genuine credentials and qualifications for hiring as a civilian Naval Intelligence agent appear to be questionable, at best. Alberti's official activities during his tenure with the Navy, and details about his subsequent, post-war life, remain limited, and shrouded in mystery.

German Rockets Destined for America

In 1947, Albert Speer, Hitler's former Architect and Minister in charge of war production, recounted Hitler's infuriation and desire to attack the United States in the closing months of the war in Europe. According to Speer:

> It was almost as if he [Hitler] was in a delirium when he described to us how New York would go up in flames. He imagined how the skyscrapers would turn into huge burning torches. How they would crumble while the reflection of the flames would light the skyline against the dark sky.

On Tuesday, April 2, 1946, *The New York Times* published a copy of a captured top-secret German map uncovered by American Intelligence Officers, entitled "How Marshal Göring Drew a Bead on New York." The map captured from Reichsmarschall Hermann Göring's files shortly after V-E Day illustrated the targeted point-of-impact for advanced V-Type rocket powered robot-bombs intended for attacks against Southern Manhattan Island, the symbolic heart of American economic and industrial might. The epicenter of the attack from multiple missiles, was located "near Delancey Street and the Bowery" (a point just 1.3 miles Northeast of the subsequently built World Trade Center towers) and designated "Zielpunkt" ("Target-

Point"), with rings indicating varied levels of destruction reaching "Central Park, the (New York) navy yard and far into Brooklyn and down the bay (the convergence of the Hudson and East Rivers)."

After the fall of the Third Reich, in June of 1945, Dr. Wernher von Braun, Dr. Ernst Steinhoff and a number of other German scientists, engineers and technicians surrendered to the Allies and under "Operation Paperclip,"[9] opted to travel to the United States. According to Annie Jacobsen, author of the book *Operation Paperclip*, on the morning of September 12, 1945, Dr. von Braun, and six other rocket engineers (including Dr. Steinhoff) were driven in jeeps from Witzenhausen Germany, to Paris. They later boarded a C-54 military transport plane and departed Europe for the United States. After refueling on the island of Santa Maria in the Azores, they landed at, and again refueled in Newfoundland, before landing at New Castle Airport in Wilmington, Delaware at 2:00 AM on September 20, 1945. From there, they boarded a second, smaller airplane and were flown to the Squantum Naval Air Station in Quincy, Massachusetts, on the South shore of Boston Harbor. At Squantum, they boarded a harbor ferry/troop transport ship that serviced the many armed forts around Boston harbor, and were landed on a gravel shoal off Nixes Mate [*sic*, actually "Nix's" Mate], a tiny island in the Harbor. From there they were transferred by a small Boston whaler type power boat the short distance across Nubble Channel to nearby Fort Strong at the Eastern tip of Long Island, where they were temporarily housed in a converted Army barracks. Dr. von Braun and Dr. Steinhoff were later taken by train to Fort Bliss, near El Paso, Texas, on October 6, 1945. From there, von Braun and Steinhoff were sent to White Sands Missile Range & Proving Ground in New Mexico, where they began testing captured German A-4/V-2s for both land and sea based applications.

Meanwhile, a team of engineers, submariners and former German rocket scientists soon assembled at the Naval Air Missile Test Center at Point Mugu, California, where they commenced the development of the U.S. Navy's first submarine launched cruise missile system (SLCM) designated the Republic JB-2 (for Jet Bomb-2) "Loon" (later re-designated the KUW-1 and the LTV-N-2). The Loon was actually just a modified surface-launched, radio-controlled German V-1 "buzz-bomb" and was first successfully launched from the U.S. Navy submarine U.S.S. *Cusk* (*SS-348*) off the coast of Point Mugu on February 12, 1947. The first controlled flight of the Loon took place on March 7, 1947, in which the missile was guided by signals from a modified submarine air-search radar-beam transmitted from the *Cusk*, before passing on control to a Navy chase plane. The initial U.S.S. *Cusk* and U.S.S. *Carbonero* (*SS-337*) LTV-N-2 Loon launch tests were carried out without the benefit of water-tight missile storage hangars, requiring the submarines to travel from their base at Point Mugu to their off-shore launch test sights while fully surfaced. It was not until the submarines were fitted with missile hangars (10' by 30' water-tight hangars mounted aft of the conning tower), that they were capable of practical deployment, at which time they could travel covertly submerged, to favorable launch sites off an enemy's coast.

On September 6, 1947 the U.S. Navy conducted a test ("Operation Sandy") in which they successfully launched a captured German A-4/V-2 rocket from the deck of the carrier U.S.S. *Midway* (*CVB-41*) "proving it was possible to fire a large missile from a rolling and pitching ship, in forward momentum." That test was followed by a 1948 test code-named "Operation Pushover" to determine what damage might occur in the event an A-4/V-2 type rocket were to topple over or misfire upon launch from a surface warship. These tests proved the hazardous undesirability of large, liquid-fueled missiles for naval applications, leaving the Loon as the only acceptable sea based, guided warhead delivery system then available. Because of the limited range and speed of the Loon, however, and the fact that it could not accommodate even the smallest nuclear warhead then available, the Navy immediately began development of a more advanced submarine launched cruise missile. The first test flight of the Vought Corp. manufactured "Regulus I" (SSM-N-8A), or so-called Regulus Attack Missile (RAM) took place in 1950. By 1954 the Regulus I (also known as "Blue Bird") had become capable of being fitted with a single, plutonium-implosion type "W-5" fission nuclear warhead with a 40 to 50 kiloton yield, as the first submarine launched, nuclear capable missile, in history. Because the Regulus armed submarines could only accommodate up to two missiles, and had to surface for significant periods of time to effectuate their launch, exposing the submarine to possible detection and attack by enemy naval and air forces, the system was soon viewed as undesirable. Consequently, naval designers and rocket scientists were once again challenged to come up with less detectable though much more lethal submarine launched ballistic missile systems for the U.S. fleet.

Simultaneously, in the 1950s captured German scientists were assisting the Soviets in the development of a submarine towed missile launch system (allegedly code-named "Golem" by NATO intelligence agencies), which had been based upon the earlier Nazi design. That Soviet project was never completed, however, opting for the more conventional submarine deck-mounted method for launching the P-5 (SS-N-3) surface-launched cruise missiles, developed under "Project 613" and deployed aboard the "Project 644" (NATO designation "Whiskey Twin Cylinder" Class) boats: *S-69*; *S-80*; *S-158*; & *S-162*. Back in the United States, research immediately began on the development of new solid-rocket propellants for use in long-range, multi-stage, submarine launched ballistic missiles. It was decided that vertical launch silo-tubes could be accommodated in the hull of large submarines, with water-tight silo-doors that could be opened for shallow, submerged launch of the missiles. It was decided that rather than risk the firing of the rocket motors while inside the submarine's hull, they could be cold-launched out of the submarine by compressed gas, with their rocket motors being ignited after safely clearing the submarine and the surface of the ocean.

U.S. Navy Admiral Hyman G. Rickover, father of the "Nuclear Navy" pioneered the construction of the Navy's first atomic powered submarine U.S.S. *Nautilus* (*SSN 571*) which was commissioned in 1954. Upon arming the Navy's newest classes of atomic powered submarines with guided "Polaris" submarine launched ballistic missiles (SLBMs) armed with atomic warheads, the nuclear submarine fleet had finally become a reality. The U.S.S. *George Washington* (*SSBN 598*), the first nuclear powered fleet ballistic missile submarine, armed with sixteen Polaris A-1 missiles, was commissioned in 1960.

Subsequent versions of the American SLBM included the ability to fit each missile with multiple warheads, each capable of precision strikes against separate targets, thousands of miles from their point of launch. These new "multiple independently-targeted reentry vehicle" (MIRV) capabilities of the "Polaris A-3," "Poseidon" and "Trident" SLBMs allowed NATO's ballistic missile fleet submarines ("Boomers") to carry significantly more warheads, with far greater strategic capabilities in the event of catastrophic international conflict. Tremendous advancements in guidance systems and targeting accuracy, or so-called "circular error probability" (CEP), the smallest diameter into which at least half the warheads would impact, also increased dramatically, allowing for lower-yield warheads which would still be capable of completely destroying an enemy target. The Steinhoff brothers' vision of an effective submarine launched missile system had truly come of age.

Dr. von Braun and Dr. Steinhoff's work was critical to the successful development of many of the United States' ballistic missile and space programs, and helped put America's first satellites and men into space, and ultimately, on the moon. Dr. von Braun and Dr. Steinhoff became United States citizens in the mid 1950s and Dr. von Braun was appointed as the Director of NASA's Marshall Space Flight Center at Huntsville, Alabama, in 1960, leading the development of the "Apollo" space program's massive "Saturn V" rocket system.

In 1980 author John Van Zwienen published a novel entitled *Pivot* (Jove Publishing; ISBN: 051505495Z), presenting a fictional account of Germany's plot to attack Manhattan with submarine launched A-4/V-2 rockets. In *Pivot,* a German spy was to have planted a radio target beacon transmitter in the Empire State Building, as the point of attack by such rockets, fitted with special radio homing guidance systems (allegedly code-named Projekt Rebstock). The rockets were to have been launched from U-boat towed, submersible launch barges, in an attempt to draw U.S. Naval resources away from the European theater. Clearly, Van Zwienen had some knowledge of Germany's 1945 plot to strike Southern Manhattan Island in a similar fashion, and his fictional account of that plot made for a truly suspenseful book. The reality of Germany's technical work toward the development of such weapons, and the important involvement of the remarkable Steinhoff brothers, is yet another example of truth being stranger than fiction.

The Steinhoff Brothers: Epilogue

On May 24, 1945 Kapitanleutnant Friedrich Steinhoff was buried by the H.L. Farmer and Son Funeral Home at the Post Cemetery on the U.S. Army base at Fort Devens in Ayer, Massachusetts (at grave marker #934), with full military honors. The *U-873* was towed to New York where she was sold for scrap and was broken up in 1948. Dr. von Braun died on June 16, 1977 in Alexandria, Virginia, and Dr. Ernst Steinhoff passed away on December 2, 1987 at the age of 79.[10]

Had the war in Europe dragged on for another year or more, with the development and construction of the Kriegsmarine's submersible rocket and missile launch containers, and the completion of the towing modifications to the Type XXI U-boats, the feared V-weapon (more probably V-1) attack on New York City might actually have transpired, spreading terror and destruction not unlike the terrorist attacks of September 11, 2001, almost six decades later. The prospect of "what might have been" grows even more alarming when considering that the *U-234* had been carrying a cargo of high grade uranium-oxide (some experts believe it was actually uranium-hexafluoride), heading for Japan. Had Germany completed development of the inter-continental A-9/A-10 rocket, and an atomic warhead suitable for that long-range delivery system, the outcome of the war may well have been changed, to that of an Axis victory.

In recent years, U.S. Navy planners have considered the possible future construction of submarine-towed, submersible weapons platforms known as the "Submarine-Towed Payload [Strike] Module" which would be capable of "increasing the submarine payload while keeping hull size down." A 1998 DARPA (Defense Advanced Research Projects Agency) study, and subsequent "Multi-Mission Module Study" in 2002 proposed a draft-board concept prototype of a system that would be capable of carrying and launching hundreds of land attack missiles. Ultimately, the German concept of submarine towed, submersible weapons platforms may also soon become a reality.

The legacy of the Steinhoff brothers could ultimately be viewed as having provided a means for the liberation of millions of oppressed peoples throughout the world. Their work led to the development of the fleet ballistic missile submarines, which were critical for the Western, free-world's Cold War triumph over the former Soviet Union, and the defeat of spreading world Communism. The silent and unseen arm of NATO's "nuclear triad" may have helped to have averted another worldwide conflict, the potential of which could have been significantly more devastating than that of even World War II, the most bloody and horrific military conflagration of all time.

The U-boat War's Final Toll

The Battle of the Atlantic began two days after Germany's September 1st 1939 invasion of Poland, when on September 3, 1939, the same day Great Britain declared war on Germany, the German Type VII U-boat *U-30* under the command of Kapitanleutnant Fritz-Julius Lemp, torpedoed and sank the British passenger liner H.M.S. *Athenia*. For more than 5 years and 8 months the deadliest naval battle in history raged across the Atlantic Ocean. The last U-boat to sink Allied shipping during the war was the *U-2336*, a Type XXIII U-boat under the command of Kapitanleutnant Emil Klausmeier on May 7th 1945 East of Dunbar, Scotland. The ships he torpedoed were the 280 foot, 1,791 ton Norwegian flagged S.S. *Sneland I* and the 2,878 ton Canadian flagged S.S. *Avondale Park*. The *U-2336* returned to Kiel and surrendered on May 14th 1945. Technically, it can be argued that the Battle of the Atlantic did not officially end until the last German U-boat, the Type VIIC *U-977* under command of Oberleutnant zur See Heinz Schaffer, surrendered at Mar del Plata, Argentina, on August 17th 1945, more that three months after Germany's surrender. Japan accepted the Allies' demand for unconditional surrender on August 14, 1945, though it was not until the declaration of surrender was signed aboard the U.S. Navy battleship U.S.S. *Missouri* (*BB-63*) in Tokyo Bay on September 2, 1945, that the war had officially come to an end.

During the war, Germany's Kriegsmarine fired nearly 38,000 torpedoes, for which its U-boats were credited with the sinking or destruction of 2,828 allied and neutral vessels including merchant freighters, tankers, military transports, passenger liners and 176 allied warships, totaling more than 14,300,000 gross tons. By comparison, during World War I from 1914 to 1918 Germany's Kaiserliche Marine U-boats sank approximately 4,837 ships totaling approximately 18 million gross tons of Allied shipping. Of the 1,162 German U-boats of varying types commissioned during World War II, 784 were sunk or destroyed. Some 429 of those U-boats were sunk without any survivors, with 215 U-boats lost on their first war patrol. Of the more than 39,000 German Kriegsmarine Officers and crewmen to serve in the U-boat service during the war, approximately 28,000 were killed and 5,000 captured, an attrition rate greater than eighty (80%) percent, higher than that sustained by any branch of any major combatant nation's military services during the war. The U.S. merchant fleet alone lost more than 700 ships sunk, with the loss of more than 5,600 merchant Officers and crewmen, while the British merchant fleet lost more than 30,000 men killed in the German U-boat campaign. Conservative estimates of the casualties incurred during the Battle of the Atlantic exceed 80,000 lives lost, including all of the Axis and Allied naval personnel, airmen, troops, merchant crewmen and civilians lost to the cold dark depths.

Though six decades have passed since the epoch Battle of the North Atlantic, the legacy of its destruction continues, as the decaying and rusting hulks of thousands of lost tankers, freighters, transports, U-boats and warships, continue to release their often poisonous and explosive cargoes into the vast ocean depths. Tens of thousands of unexploded depth-charges, hedgehogs, mines and torpedoes remain hazardous to those unfortunate enough to come across them. On July 23, 1965 Captain Edward Doodley of Portland, Maine, aboard the fishing vessel (scallop dragger) "*Snoopy*," hauled aboard a heavy, elongated object in his nets while trawling off the

North Carolina coast. Captain Doodley radioed his find to the nearby New Bedford fishing trawler *Prowler,* and only moments later the *Snoopy* disappeared in a tremendous explosion. Apparently, the *Snoopy* had dragged up an old, though still live, armed and highly volatile German torpedo in her nets. Of the 12 crewmen aboard the *Snoopy* at the time of the detonation, only four badly injured crewmen survived to be rescued. Of the eight crewmen killed, only the body of Captain Doodley was recovered.

The Steinhoff family circa 1918, from left to right: mother, Augusta; sons Ernst, Ludwig II and Friedrich; and father, Ludwig. (Courtesy of Monika Steinhoff-O'Friel)

Friedrich Steinhoff graduated from the Kriegsmarine training academy with the Class of 1935 at the age of 26. This is Kapitanleutnant Steinhoff at about the time he assumed command of the Type IXC U-boat *U-511* in December of 1941 at the age of 32. (Courtesy of Monika Steinhoff-O'Friel)

Six solid propellant 30 centimeter diameter (11.8 inch) Wurfkorper 24 Speng (Rocket, Model 42) German Army artillery rockets in a jerry-rigged frame mounting six Schweres Wurfgerat 41 launch racks. This elongated frame was later disassembled and reconstructed in a much shorter, more compact configuration, before being mounted on the aft deck of the Type IXC U-boat *U-511*. (Courtesy of the late Horst Bredow, Curator at the U-Boot-Archiv at Cuxhaven-Altenbruch, Germany)

The Wurfkorper 24 Speng artillery rockets being erected above the aft deck of the U-boat *U-511* under command of Kapitanleutnant Friedrich Steinhoff, at Germany's secret rocket test center at Peenemunde, on the Baltic Sea, prior to the successful test launch on June 4, 1942. (Courtesy of the late Horst Bredow, Curator at the U-Boot-Archiv at Cuxhaven-Altenbruch, Germany)

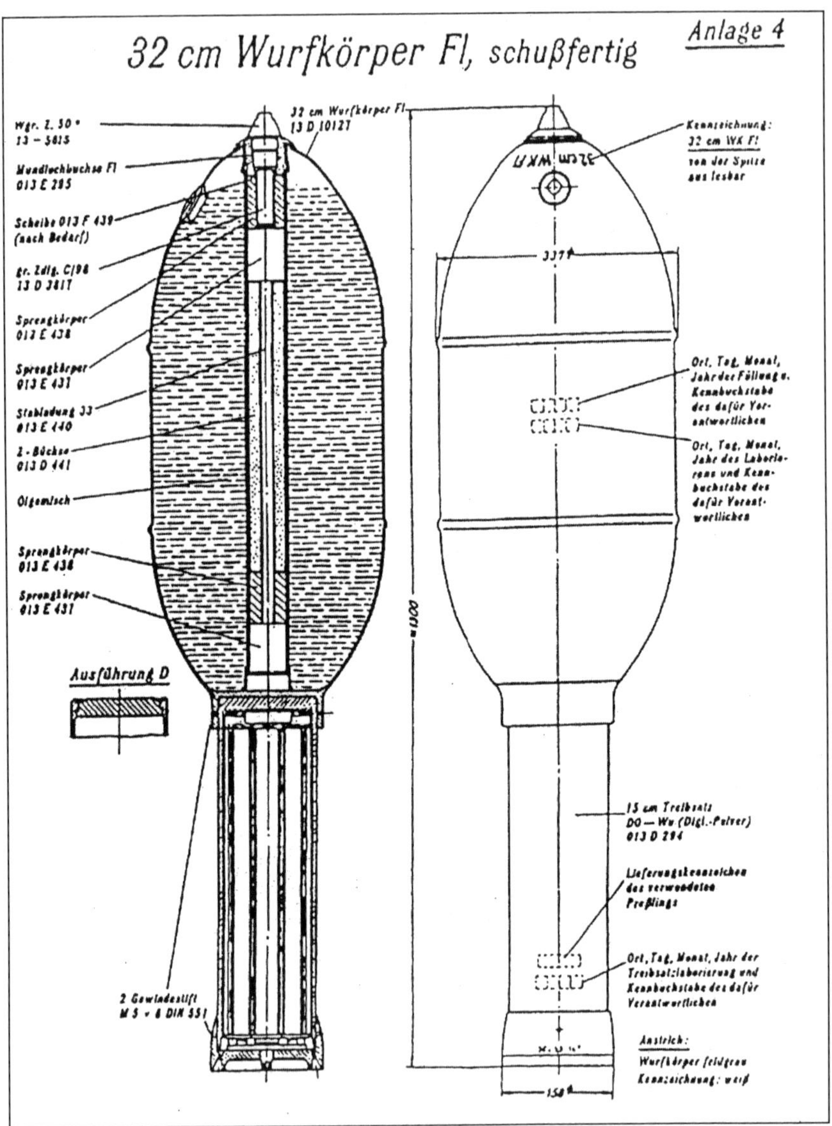

Cross-section of a solid propellant 32 centimeter rocket similar to the 30 centimeter diameter (11.8 inch) Wurfkorper 24 Speng (Rocket, Model 42) German Army artillery rocket, the basis for the slightly modified "Do-38" submarine launched missile developed under "Projekt Ursel." Each rocket was approximately 4 feet in length and weighed 279.4 pounds including a 98.3 pound high-explosive warhead. Traveling at a velocity of 754 feet per second, they had a range of 4,960 yards, or approximately 2.8 miles. (Courtesy of the National Archives)

Doktor (Doctor) Ernst Steinhoff standing (to the right of the periscope) on the aft "wintergarten" (winter-garden), the raised gun platform aft of the conning-tower of the U-boat *U-511*. To his right is the world's leading rocket scientist Professor Dr. Wernher von Braun, and just to the right of von Braun, wearing the white Commanders cap, is Kapitanleutnant Friedrich Steinhoff just prior to their first successful submerged rocket test launch which took place on June 4, 1942. (Courtesy of Dr. Frank Steinhoff)

Photo of the submerged Type IXC U-boat *U-511* under command of Kapitanleutnant Friedrich Steinhoff, conducting the first successful submerged test launch of Wurfkorper 24 Speng (Rocket, Model 42) German Army artillery rockets, off the coast of Germany's secret rocket test center at Peenemunde, on the Baltic Sea, on June 4, 1942. (Courtesy of the late Horst Bredow, Curator at the U-Boot-Archiv at Cuxhaven-Altenbruch, Germany)

Kapitanleutnant Friedrich Steinhoff and several Officers and crewmen aboard the Type IXC U-boat *U-511*, celebrate the successful rocket test launch from his submerged submarine on June 4, 1942, with shots of schnapps. (Courtesy of the late Horst Bredow, Curator at the U-Boot-Archiv at Cuxhaven-Altenbruch, Germany)

Kapitanleutnant Friedrich Steinhoff and his Officers and crewmen mustered aboard the new long-range Type IXD-2 "U-Cruiser" U-boat, *U-873* at the AG Weser shipyard at Bremen, Germany, upon her Commissioning on March 1, 1944 (Courtesy of Dr. Frank Steinhoff)

Kapitanleutnant Friedrich Steinhoff and his Officers and crewmen mustered aboard the U-boat, *U-873* at the AG Weser shipyard at Bremen, Germany, upon her Commissioning on March 1, 1944. (Courtesy of Dr. Frank Steinhoff)

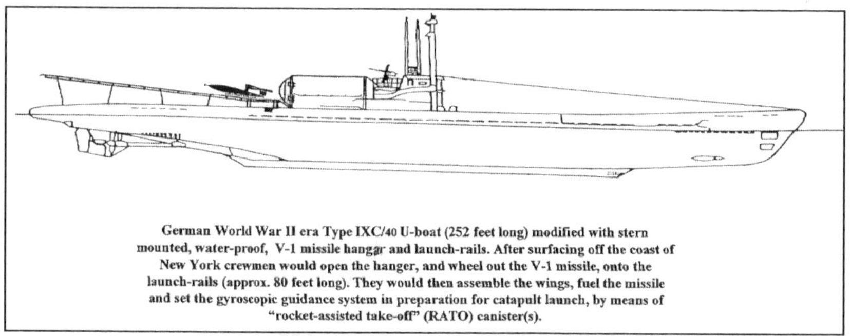

German World War II era Type IXC/40 U-boat (252 feet long) modified with stern mounted, water-proof, V-1 missile hangar and launch-rails. After surfacing off the coast of New York crewmen would open the hanger, and wheel out the V-1 missile, onto the launch-rails (approx. 80 feet long). They would then assemble the wings, fuel the missile and set the gyroscopic guidance system in preparation for catapult launch, by means of "rocket-assisted take-off" (RATO) canister(s).

The author's diagram of a concept-prototype German Type IXC/40 U-boat modified with a stern mounted, waterproof, V-1 "Fieseler Fi-103" (V-1) pulse-jet powered, guided cruise-type missile, or so-caller "Buzz-Bomb" or "Doodle-Bug" missile hangar and launch rails. The launch rails have been erected and the V-1 rolled-out, onto it with the wings attached in preparation for launch. (Illustration by the author)

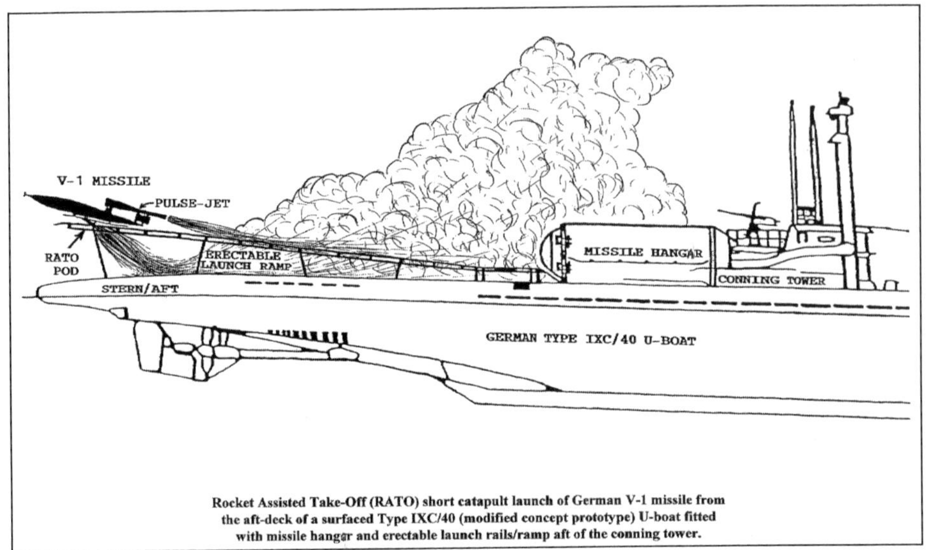

Rocket Assisted Take-Off (RATO) short catapult launch of German V-1 missile from the aft-deck of a surfaced Type IXC/40 (modified concept prototype) U-boat fitted with missile hangar and erectable launch rails/ramp aft of the conning tower.

The author's diagram of a German Type IXC/40 U-boat modified with a waterproof hangar and V-1 launch equipment at the moment of a Rocket-Assisted Take-Off (RATO)short catapult launch from the stern of a Type IXC/40 U-boat. (Illustration by the author)

1727

Geheime Kommandosache!

Chef-Sache
Nur durch Offizier

Nr. 94/44 gKdos. Chefs

Nr. 1357

O.U., den 11. Dezember 1944.

4 Ausfertigungen
1. Ausfertigung: General Rossmann
2. Ausfertigung: Direktor Riedel III, E.W.
3. Ausfertigung: Dr. Dickmann, Vulkan Werft
4. Ausfertigung: Entwurf, Wa Prüf (BuM) 10/I

N i e d e r s c h r i f t

über die Besprechung vom 9.12.1944 bei Wa Prüf (BuM) 10.

Teilnehmer: Wa Prüf (BuM) 10:

Generalmajor	Rossmann	Abt.Chef
Oberstltn.	Börgemann	Abt.Chef z.b.V.
Major	Schneider	Gruppenleiter I
Dr.Ing.	Jauernick	für Gruppenl.II
Major	Wenzel	Gruppenl.III
Hauptmann	Hofmann	Gruppenl.IV
Oberinspekt.	Schuchmann	für Gruppenl.V

Vulkan Werft Stettin: Dr. Dickmannn

E.W. Karlshagen:

Direktor	Riedel III
Direktor	Hüter
Dipl.Ing.	Lührsen
Dr.	Debus

Gegenstand der Besprechung:

Schiessen mit A4 von See aus.

Zweck der Besprechung:

Erste technische Fühlungnahme zwischen der Werft und der Entwicklungsabteilung des Gerätes. Vorklärung und Fixierung einiger grundlegender Fragen über die schiesstechnische Durchführbarkeit des Vorhabens.

Inhalt der Besprechung:

Dr. Dickmann erläutert den Plan, das Gerät A4 in einem von einem U-Boot unter Wasser geschleppten Schwimmkörper auf günstige Schussposition auf eine feindliche Küste heranzubringen, das Gerät von dem in Schussstellung gebrachten Schwimmkörper zu verschiessen und diesen zu neuer Verwendung wieder zum Heimathafen zurückzuschleppen. Schiffsbaumässig ergeben sich hier vor allem die Abmessungen, der geforderten Stabilität und weiterer, durch die Fragen der Eigenarten des Gerätes und des Abschusses beding-ten Einrichtungen.

The so-called "Dickmann Letter" setting forth the idea behind the development of submarine towed, submersible launch containers from which V-2 ballistic missiles might be transported across the Atlantic Ocean to bombard American coastal cities and military installations. (Courtesy of the National Archives)

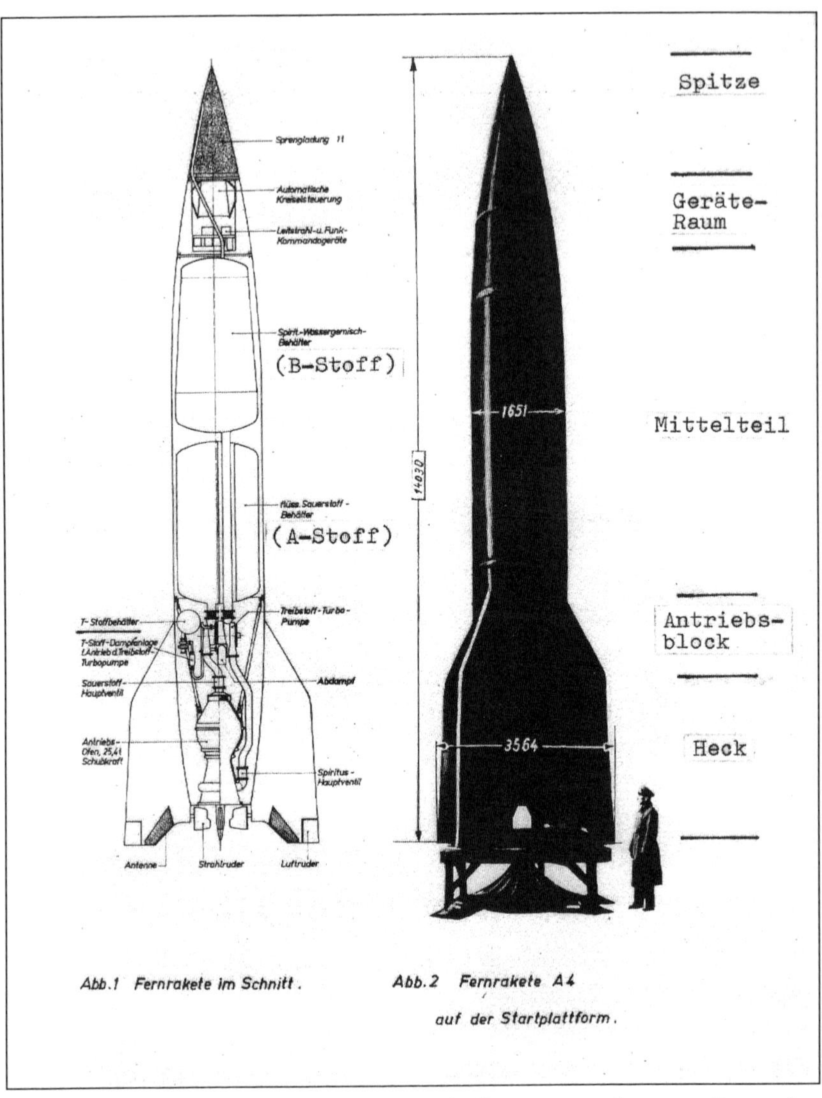

Cross-section of a German A-4 (V-2) ballistic missile. Standing 46 feet tall and weighing in at approximately 12 tons fully fueled it had a range in excess of 200 miles and carried a one-ton warhead. It was planned to be carried aboard a submarine towed, submersible silo launching barge to an area off the American Northeast coast and fired into southern Manhattan, New York. (Courtesy of the New Mexico Museum of Space History).

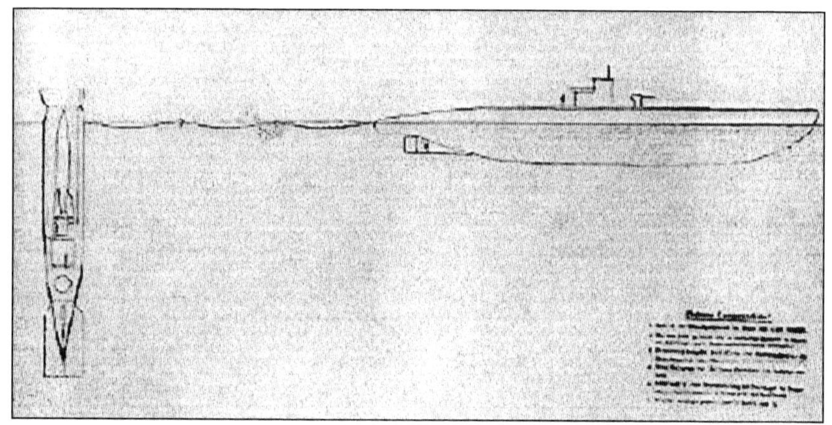

A crudely drafted illustration that accompanied the "Dickmann Letter" showing roughly how a U-boat would tow and prepare a submersible V-2 launch container, later to become known as "Apparatus-F" to the American East coast, to attack such targets as New York City. (Courtesy of the National Archives)

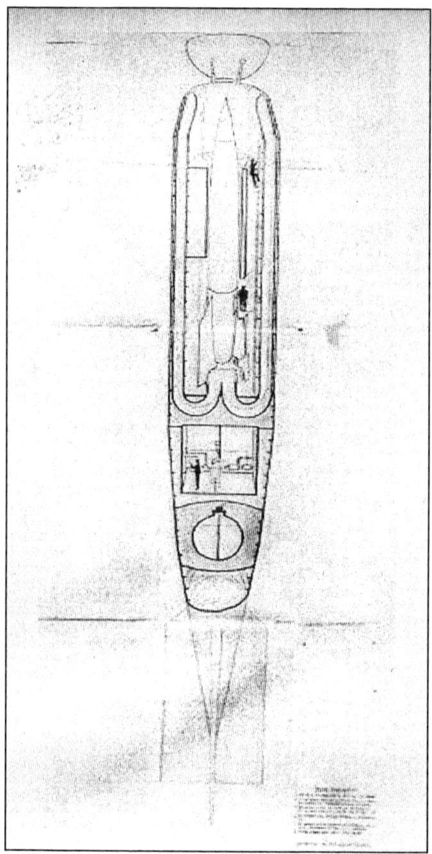

A crudely drafted illustration that accompanied the "Dickmann Letter" showing roughly how a U-boat towed, submersible V-2 launch container, later to become known as "Apparatus-F," was to have been manned, partially flooded and inverted to perpendicular, in preparation for launch. (Courtesy of the National Archives)

A one-third (1/3) scale mock-up of a submarine towed, submersible container fabricated for towing trials at AG Vuncan Weft, one of several built for testing in preparation for the fabrication of the full-size Apparatus-F, V-2 (A-4) launch containers. (Courtesy of the late Horst Bredow, Curator at the U-Boot-Archiv at Cuxhaven-Altenbruch, Germany)

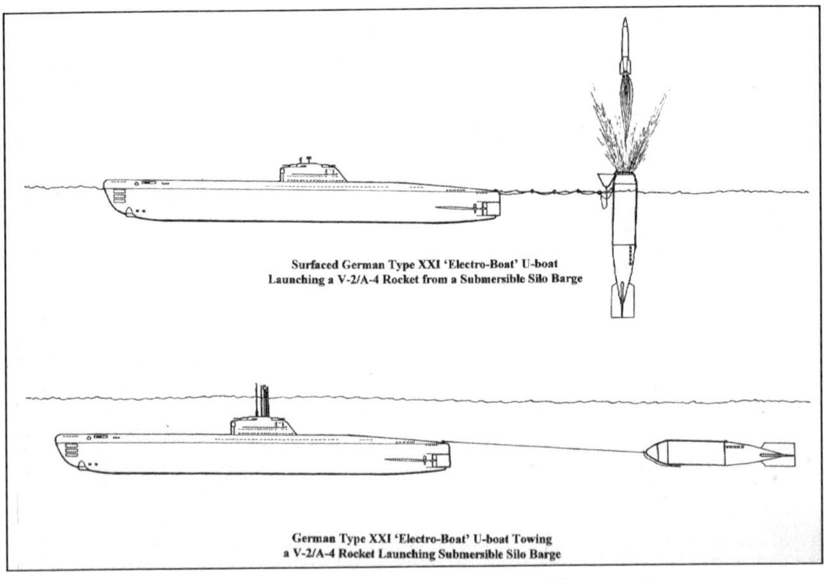

The author's diagram of a 300 ton submersible "underwater lighter-barge" or "rocket-silo- barge" known as Apparatus-F, armed with a V-2 (A-4) ballistic missile. Shown in the submerged, towing configuration (bottom) and stopped at the launch site, with the aft section of Apparatus-F having been flooded and inverted, with bow cap open, in the launch position. (Illustration by the author)

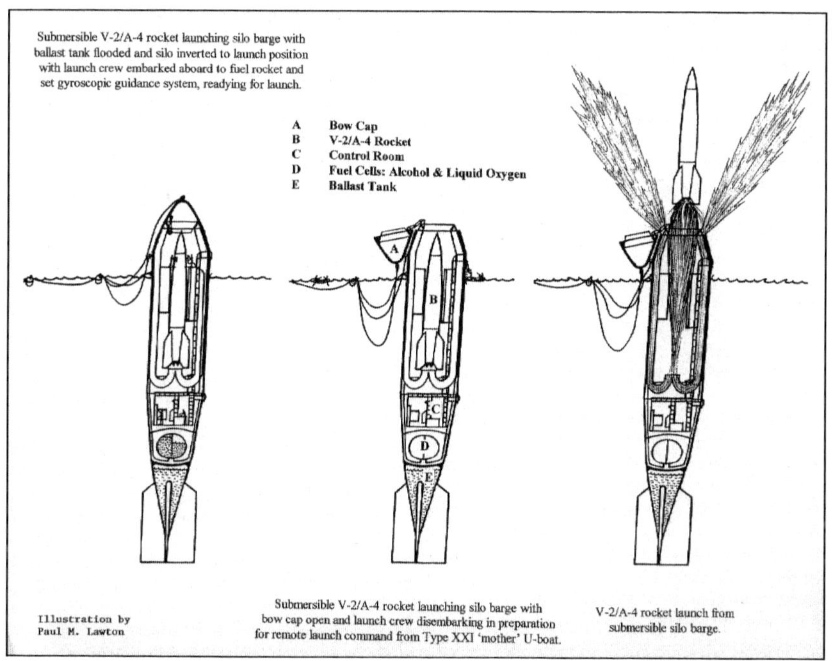

The author's diagram of a 300 ton submersible "rocket-silo-barge" known as Apparatus-F armed with a V-2 (A-4) ballistic missile. Towed behind a German U-boat, the launch container is shown with the aft section flooded, and inverted to the launch position, with: (on left) crewmen embarked on board to fuel the rocket and set the gyroscopic guidance system in preparation for launch; (center) bow cap open and launch crewmen disembarking to return to the mother ship; (right) the V-2 (A-4) being launched. (Illustration by the author)

Photograph of Kapitanleutnant Friedrich Steinhoff, Commander of the Type IXD- 2 German U-boat, *U-873* after surrendering his boat. Taken on Wednesday, May 17, 1945 at the Portsmouth (New Hampshire) U.S. Navy Base. Steinhoff is seen under U.S. Marine armed guard before being transferred by bus to Boston. (Photograph courtesy of Clint Winslow, former Officer aboard the U.S. Coast Guard Cutter USCGC Argo)

The ominous Portsmouth Naval Prison at the Portsmouth, New Hampshire Navy Base where Kapitanleutnant Steinhoff surrendered the *U-873*. Commander Steinhoff underwent his initial "interview" in a dungeon like isolation cell known as "The Pit" in the Portsmouth Naval Prison, conducted by a special interrogation team of the U.S. Navy's Office of Naval Intelligence known as "Op-16-Z." (Courtesy of the author)

BASIC PERSONNEL RECORD
(Alien Enemy or Prisoner of War)

1G-445 NA (Internment serial number)

STEINHOFF, Fritz (Name of internee)

M (Sex)

Height 1.83 m ft. in.

Weight 60 K

Eyes Blue

Skin Ruddy

Hair Blond

Age 35

Distinguishing marks or characteristics:

1G 445 NA

1G 445 NA

F. P. C.*

Reference*

INVENTORY OF PERSONAL EFFECTS TAKEN FROM INTERNEE

1.
2.
3.
4.
5.
6.
7.
8.
9.

The above is correct: Steinhoff (Signature of internee)

(Date and place where processed (Army enclosure, naval station, or other place))

RIGHT HAND

1. Thumb	2. Index finger	3. Middle finger	4. Ring finger	5. Little finger

LEFT HAND

6. Thumb	7. Index finger	8. Middle finger	9. Ring finger	10. Little finger

W. D., P. M. G. Form No. 2 21 June 1943 — Note Amputation in Proper Space — * Do not fill in.

Basic Personnel Record: Alien Enemy or Prisoner of War photograph, fingerprint and information card for Kapitanleutnant Friedrich [*sic*] "Fritz" Steinhoff from his intake at the Portsmouth Naval Prison on May 17, 1945. The card was back dated to May 11th, the actual day the U-873 surrendered at sea to U.S. Navy forces.

U.S. Navy Office of Naval Intelligence (ONI) Op-16-Z photo of Jach Henry Alberti, the Belgian national recruited by the Navy as a civilian Naval Intelligence agent who was known to masquerade around dressed in the uniform of a Lieutenant Commander of the U.S. Navy and to use the alias "Alvares." As a "Chief Interrogator" of German Navy PoWs, he was known to use so-called "shock interrogation" techniques including violent physical coercion in order to extract information in violation of the Geneva Convention protocols. (Both courtesy of Bernard Cavalcante)

The Commonwealth of Massachusetts
OFFICE OF THE SECRETARY
DIVISION OF VITAL STATISTICS
MEDICAL EXAMINER'S
CERTIFICATE OF DEATH

1 PLACE OF DEATH: SUFFOLK (County); BOSTON (City or Town)
No. en route to Mass. Gen'l Hosp. St. (If death occurred in a hospital or institution, give its NAME instead of street and number)

2 FULL NAME Fritz Steinhoff (If deceased is a married, widowed or divorced woman, give also maiden name.)
(Was deceased a U. S. War Veteran, if so specify WAR)

(a) Residence, No. Germany (Usual place of abode) St. (If nonresident, give city or town and State)

Length of stay: In hospital or institution ... years months days. In this community yrs. mos. days (Before death) (Specify whether)

PERSONAL AND STATISTICAL PARTICULARS	MEDICAL CERTIFICATE OF DEATH
3 SEX: Male. 4 COLOR OR RACE: white. 5 SINGLE, MARRIED, WIDOWED or DIVORCED (write the word): Unknown	18 DATE OF DEATH: May 19, 1945 (Month) (Day) (Year)
5a If married, widowed, or divorced HUSBAND of (Give maiden name of wife in full) (or) WIFE of (Husband's name in full)	19 I HEREBY CERTIFY that I have investigated the death of the person above-named and that the CAUSE AND MANNER thereof are as follows: (If an injury was involved, state fully.) Incised wound right wrist
6 Age of husband or wife if alive ... years	xxxxxxxxxxxxxxx
7 IF STILLBORN, enter that fact here.	
8 AGE 25 ? Years Months Days. If less than 1 day ... Hours ... Minutes	20 Accident, suicide, or homicide (specify) Suicidal. Date of occurrence May 19, 1946
9 Usual Occupation: Officer (Submarine)	Where did injury occur? Boston (City or town and State)
10 Industry or Business: German Army	Did injury occur in or about home, on farm, in industrial place, or in public place? Jail (Specify type of place)
11 Social Security No.	Manner of Injury: Found bleeding while a prisoner
12 BIRTHPLACE (City) (State or country) ------	Nature of Injury: or at Charles St Jail May 19/45
13 NAME OF FATHER ------	While at work? ---- Was there an autopsy? Yes
14 BIRTHPLACE OF FATHER (City) (State or country) ------	21 Was disease or injury in any way related to occupation of deceased? If so, specify
15 MAIDEN NAME OF MOTHER ------	(Signed) W J Brickley M. D. (Address) Boston Mass Date 6-19 1945
16 BIRTHPLACE OF MOTHER (City) (State or country) ------	22 Post Cem-Fort Devens. Place of Burial, Cremation or Removal (City or Town)
17 Informant Hosp Records (Address) Relation, if any	DATE OF BURIAL May 24/45
I HEREBY CERTIFY that a satisfactory standard certificate of death was filed with me BEFORE the burial or transit permit was issued:	23 NAME OF FUNERAL DIRECTOR H L Farmer & Son. ADDRESS Ayer Mass
(Signature of Agent of Board of Health or other)	Received and filed May 25/45
(Official Designation) (Date of Issue of Permit)	A TRUE COPY ATTEST: (Registrar)

Kapitanleutnant Friedrich Steinhoff's Death Certificate from the office of the Massachusetts State Medical Examiner listing the cause of death as "suicide" and the manner of death as "Incised wound right wrist." Under that was an excised entry that had been crossed out (ex-ed out). What the exact nature of that redacted entry might have been may never be known. (Courtesy of the Massachusetts State Medical Examiner's Office)

Suffolk County's Charles Street Jail (marked "A") in Boston, where Kapitanleutnant Friedrich Steinhoff was found unconscious and bleeding from an alleged self-inflicted wound on the morning of May 19, 1945. Immediately behind the jail is the George Robert White Memorial Building at the Massachusetts General Hospital (marked "B") which was built in 1939 and looked much like it does today. Though the hospital was only yards away, Commander Steinhoff was denied medical treatment for two and a half hours, allowing him to pass away, when he otherwise could have been saved. (Courtesy of the author)

Kapitanleutnant Friedrich Steinhoff's grave at the U.S. Army base at Fort Devens in Ayer, Massachusetts, where he was buried with full military honors. (Courtesy of Jim Fahey)

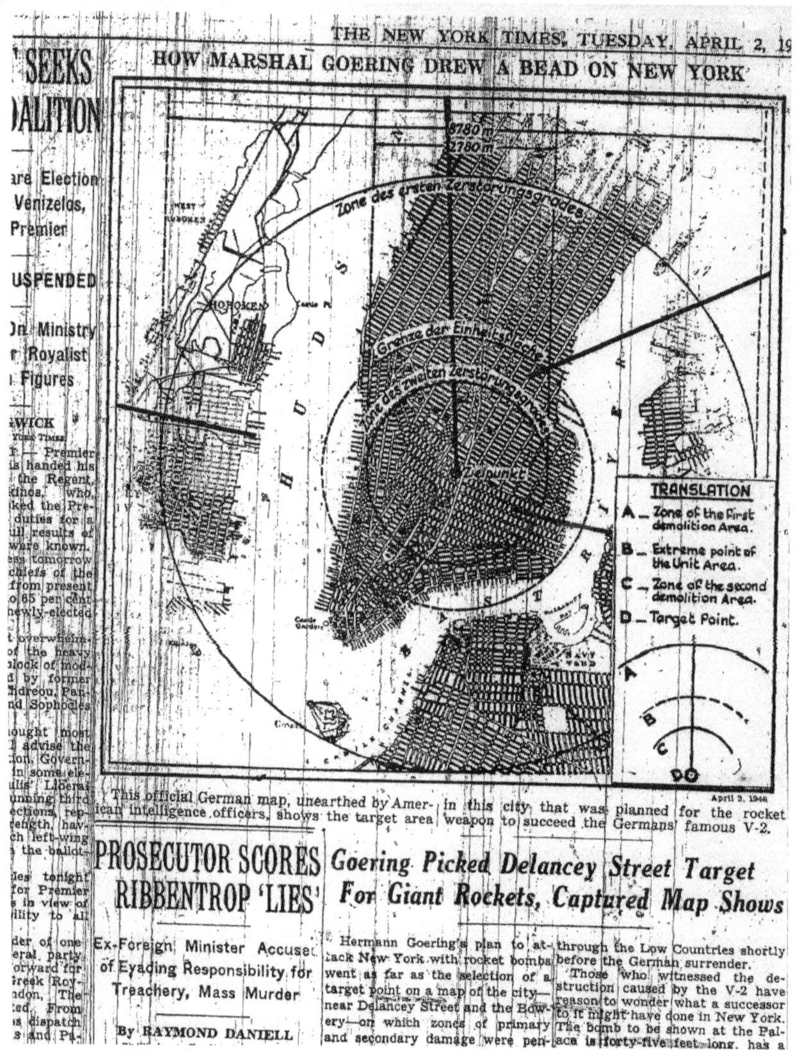

THE NEW YORK TIMES, TUESDAY, APRIL 2, 19

SEEKS
...ALITION

...are Election
Venizelos,
Premier

...USPENDED

...on Ministry
...r Royalist
...Figures

HOW MARSHAL GOERING DREW A BEAD ON NEW YORK

April 2, 1946

This official German map, unearthed by American intelligence officers, shows the target area in this city that was planned for the rocket weapon to succeed the Germans' famous V-2.

PROSECUTOR SCORES RIBBENTROP 'LIES'

Ex-Foreign Minister Accused of Evading Responsibility for Treachery, Mass Murder

By RAYMOND DANIELL

Goering Picked Delancey Street Target For Giant Rockets, Captured Map Shows

Hermann Goering's plan to attack New York with rocket bombs went as far as the selection of a target point on a map of the city—near Delancey Street and the Bowery—on which zones of primary and secondary damage were pen-

through the Low Countries shortly before the German surrender.

Those who witnessed the destruction caused by the V-2 have reason to wonder what a successor to it might have done in New York. The bomb to be shown at the Palace is forty-five feet long. has a

Copy of the Tuesday, April 2, 1946 issue of *The New York Times* showing a captured top-secret German map uncovered by American Intelligence Officers, entitled "How Marshal Göring Drew a Bead on New York." The map captured from Reichsmarschall Hermann Göring's files shortly after V-E Day illustrated the targeted point-of-impact for advanced V-Type rocket powered "robot-bombs" intended for attacks against Southern Manhattan Island. That same target point, the symbolic heart of American economic and industrial strength was ultimately attacked by another enemy of the United States, on September 11th 2001, almost six decades later.

Regulus I Submarine Launched Cruise Missile (SLCM) being loaded aboard the U.S. Navy submarine U.S.S. *Tunny*, in the early 1950s. Had Germany held out long enough during World War II to deploy their "Fieseler Fi-103" (V-1) "Buzz- Bombs" for launch by U-boats, they likely would have employed a similar configuration. (Courtesy of the United States Navy)

Dr. Ernst Steinhoff citca the late 1970s a Chief Scientist of the U.S. Air Force Missile Development Center at Holloman Air Force Base and as Director of the New Mexico Research Institute. In 1935, in Germany, he set the world's record for solo, long distance, cross-country sail-plane (glider) flight of 314 miles for which he was bestowed the honorary rank of "Flight Captain" in the German air force (Luftwaffe), sport he continued to enjoy well into his elder years in the United Stated (Courtesy of Monika Steinhoff-O'Friel).

HITLER'S
RAKETEN U-BOOTE
(Rocket-Submarine)
From German Secret Weapon
to the
Ballistic Missile Submarine

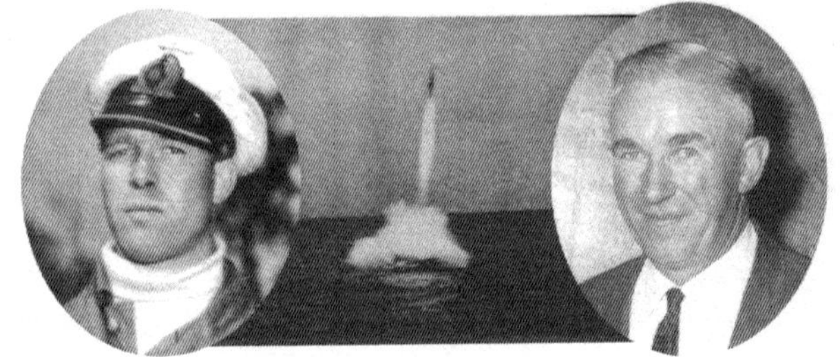

The Untold Legacy
of the
Steinhoff Brothers

By Paul M. Lawton, Esquire
Naval Historian

The cover to the author's original, self-published research monograph entitled *Hitler's Raketen U-Boote,* which was generously donated to dozens of air and space and military museums in the U.S., Great Britain and Germany in the late 1990s. Though the author did not copyright this work until 2001, it was translated into German and made part of the permanent research collections of such institutions as the State Library in Wurttemberg in Stuttgart and the Deutsches U-Boot-Museun in Cuxhaven-Altenbruch as well as the Smithsonian National Air & Space Museum in Washington, D.C., and the New Mexico Museum of Space History at Alamogordo, New Mexico, in the U.S. It has alternately been filed at different institutions under different titles including, most recently: *Wunderwaffen: U-511, U-1063 und die Pläne für U-Boote mit seegestützen Raketen* (Wonder-Weapon: *U-511, U-1063* and the Plan for U-boats with Sea-Launched Rockets). (Courtesy of the author)

Endnotes

1. While docked in a Norwegian harbor Commander Steinhoff's minesweeper was attacked by Allied aircraft, and was struck on the quarterdeck by an aerial bomb and sunk, but not before his crew shot down the attacking aircraft with the ship's anti-aircraft guns. Though the Kriegsmarine determined the ship to be a total loss, and had no intention on raising her, Steinhoff insisted on her salvage, and prevailing upon higher authorities, the ship was raised, repaired, re-commissioned and returned to active service.

2. Technically, it can be argued that the first, though unintended successful launch of a so-called "missile" (though not a "rocket") from a submarine, actually took place in the United States circa 1881. American submarine pioneer John Holland conducted trials with his gasoline powered "*Fenian Ram*" submarine, by outfitting it with an experimental 11 foot long pneumatic torpedo launch tube, from which a 6 foot long, 9 inch diameter torpedo (actually not self-propelled but more of a projectile), was fired under 300 pounds per square inch (psi) of pressure. Because of improper ballasting, however, the experimental torpedo had the tendency to rise to the surface immediately after launch, often leaving the water and flying through the air. On at least one occasion while test firing in New Jersey's Morris Canal Basin the *Fenian Ram* fired a torpedo from a depth of only 3 feet, and according to witnesses, after clearing the tube by only 8 to 10 feet the torpedo broke the surface and flew 60 to 70 feet through the air before crashing back into the water and burying itself in the mud.

3. "Operation Pastorius" was Germany's code-name for the landing of eight "Abwehr" (German Intelligence Service) spies and saboteurs, four each from the Type VIIC U-boats *U-202* (*KL* Hans Heinz Linder); and *U-584* (*KL* Joachim Deeks) on the coasts of Amagansett, Long Island, New York, and Ponte Verda, Florida on June 13th and 16th of 1942, respectively. All eight spies were later captured, tried and convicted of espionage and sabotage, with six being executed by electric-chair in Washington, DC on August 8, 1942.

4. Submarines designed to carry and launch small aircraft stored in deck-mounted, water-tight hangars, were commonly tested and deployed by major nations just prior to World War II. Aircraft-carrying submarines included the American *S-1*; British *M-2*; French "*Surcouf*"; Italian "*Ettore Fieramosca*"; and the Japanese *I-400* class.

5. Germany's secret "Fieseler Fi-103" (also designated the FZG-76) "Vergeltungswaffe-Eins" or Vengeance Weapon One (V-1) pulse-jet powered, guided cruise-type missile, known by the British as the so-caller "Buzz-Bomb" or "Doodle-Bug" the first of Germany's operational "Vengeance" weapons, was developed at the Argus Motorwerke Gesellschaft. At 27 feet long and just under 5 feet in diameter, it was gasoline powered (by a single Argus As 109-14 pulse-jet motor) and rail-launched. The V-1's land-based launch propulsion unit employed the Heinkel steam generator known as a "Kinderwagen" (baby-carriage) which used a Walther hydrogen-peroxide fuel mixture to generate steam pressure to drive the missile up and off the launch-ramp. The standard land-based V-1 launch ramp was 48 meters (approx. 150 feet) long, with a six (6) degree angle of inclination and five (5) meters (approx. 15 ft.) high at the end. Because of the limited length of the launch-rails that could have been fitted aboard a U-boat, however, the sea-launched version of the V-1 missile

would likely have employed smokeless, solid-propellant, rocket-assisted take-off (RATO) canisters (they are often erroneously referred to as JATO canisters for "Jet" assisted take off, though they were actually rocket, rather than jet powered).

For carrying aboard, and launching from a U-boat, a water-tight missile hangar (measuring approximately 35 feet long by 15 feet in diameter), would have to have been fitted to the deck just behind the conning tower, with an approximately 80 foot launch-ramp used for firing the V-1 missile off the stern. At 4,800 pounds, it carried a one ton high explosive warhead consisting of trinitrotoluol and ammonium nitrate. With an average speed of just over 400 miles-per-hour, it flew at pre-set altitudes of between 1,000 and 7,000 feet, with a range of up to 250 miles. Germany's V-1 is considered to be the predecessor of all modern cruise missiles. Much simpler in construction, the V-1 was also considerably less expensive to manufacture compared to Germany's V-2 rocket.

Germany's secret "Vergeltungswaffe-Zwei" Vengeance Weapon Two V-2 (German designation "A-4") guided-rocket, or so-called "robot bomb" was 46 feet tall, and 5 feet 5 inches in diameter, weighing approximately 4 tons un-fueled and 12.5 tons at launch, 70 percent being fuel weight. Fueled by 11,000 pounds of liquid oxygen (called "A-Stoff" or "A-Substance" by the Germans), and 8,300 pounds of ethyl-alcohol ("B-Stoff"), it consumed its oxidized fuel at a rate of 275 pounds-per-second, for approximately seventy (70) seconds of burn-time, through which the rocket traveled just 25% of its actual ballistic trajectory. The A-4/V-2's fuel was fed by a small but extremely powerful 600 horse-power, hot steam/oxygen generated turbine-fuel-pump, which itself was fueled by hydrogen-peroxide (H_2O_2) a/k/a ("T-Stoff"), and the heated liquid catalyst sodium-permanganate ("Z-Stoff"). With a one ton warhead, the V-2's guidance system included two, three-axis gyroscopic stabilizers, making it accurate enough to target an enemy city at ranges in excess of 200 miles. The V-2's combustion chamber generated between 25,000 to 26,000 kilograms (55,110 to 57,320 pounds) of thrust, the rocket was capable of speeds of more than 4,000 miles-per-hour, could reach altitudes of up to 55 miles (space flight is considered to begin at approximately 62 miles in altitude), and could travel from Holland to London, England, in just four minutes. Approximately 5,400 V-2s were manufactured before the end of the war (of which approximately 3,600 were fired against the Allies), at an average cost of 75,000 Reichmarks per unit (The first production A-4/V-2 cost 1.5 million Reichmarks, but final production costs had been reduced to 37,000 Reichmarks), with each taking up to 13,000 man-hours to fabricate. Each A-4/V-2 rocket contained some 17,000 individual parts, and during peak production (primarily enabled by slave labor provided by the nearby concentration camp "Dora"), Germany's secret underground factory at Nordhausen (also known as Mittelwerk) in the Harz Mountains, was turning out as many as 13 rockets per day.

The first German "Vengeance Weapon" to be employed against London was the Luftwaffe's V-1, which because of its subsonic speed and relatively low flight altitude, was highly susceptible to interception and destruction by Allied fighter aircraft and anti-aircraft cannon fire. Of 8,564 V-1s fired against London, only about 2,400 actually reached the city. The A-4/V-2, however, with its high speed and elliptical trajectory, made it impossible to be intercepted with weapons of that time. Rarely seen and never heard before their impact, of the approximately 1,200 A-4/V-2s launched against London in the eight month period between September 4, 1944 and March 27, 1945, none were ever intercepted.

By the war's end German scientists were working on the development of a gigantic, two-stage rocket (the second-stage being a modified version of the A-4/V-2) designated the **"A-9/A-10"** (A-9/10), which would have been the first intercontinental ballistic missile. The A-9 (aka the A-4b) was actually a winged-version of the A-4/V-2, mounted on a massive first stage booster (estimated to generate 180,000 kilograms of thrust, and 50 seconds of burn time) designated the A-10, which would lift the A-9 into the stratosphere before separating and allowing the A-9 to fire its second stage, lifting it further to the edge of space (calculated ceiling of 350 kilometers), where it would then glide to the distant target. Estimated to have been capable of a range of 5,500 kilometers (3,400+ miles), had the 200 ton, 87 foot tall A-9/A-10 been launched from Western Europe, it would have been able to attack a number of major cities along the American Northeast coast. Particular scrutiny was given to the guidance challenges posed by sea launched (or ultra-long-range European land lunched) missiles and rockets against precise land targets. There was some discussion about the possibility of having German agents landed near the New York coast, where they would travel to Manhattan Island and set up radio transmitter beacons that guided rockets or missiles could home-in on. Such an arrangement would have required the development of a radio-homing guidance system for installation aboard the V-1 missiles or A-4/V-2 rockets, and would have taken over guidance during the terminal ballistic trajectory of the weapon as it approached the intended target.

On May 18, 1945, Professor (Dr.) von Braun told members of the U.S. Navy's Technical Mission interrogation team of another method for the terminal guidance of Germany's long-range ballistic rocket, stating that: "the A-9/A-10 combination could be piloted to a landing, the pilot taking over the controls as the atmosphere is reached on the downward trajectory." Dr. von Braun did not make it clear as to whether the pilot would be guiding the rocket on a suicide mission (typical terminal velocity of the A-4/V-2 would have made a survivable bail-out impossible, but for the potential capabilities of the winged, glider version A-9), or whether arrangements would be made for the pilot to bail out and parachute to earth before impact. It appears that the latter scenario had been considered, as the Technical Mission report stated that: "Von Braun felt that normal airplane landing speeds could be achieved." In a rather shocking revelation, the Technical Mission report also added:

> It was even proposed to build a rocket [Note: Dr. von Braun was describing the hypervelocity, stratospheric "Silber Vogel" (Silver Bird) rocket-bomber designed by Austrian rocket engineer, Dr. Eugen Sanger] to fly from Germany to New York, bomb from the stratosphere, turn around, return and make a landing in Germany.

The Silver Bird was intended to deliver a 5,000 pound high explosive gravity bomb encased in a shell of highly irradiated silica (radioactive sand), constituting the first proposed tactical use of a so-called "Radiological" or "Dirty-Bomb."

6. In fairness to Commander Steinhoff, it was a common, though often inaccurate term for American and Allied military personnel to refer to all German combatants as "Nazis," since most were not actually members of the Nazi party. Germany's World War II era Nazi party was not an open political party that anyone could simply choose to join, as are most modern, free world political parties. Germany's Nazi party was a closed, exclusive group, reserved for the rich, powerful, and influential ideologues, and their status was bestowed with certain privileges not enjoyed by the general populous. Consequently, many of the millions of Germany's uniformed military personnel, though highly patriotic and nationalistic, were not necessarily members of the

Nazi party, and many did not study, nor even fully understand the dogmas of National Socialism. Commander Friedrich Steinhoff was not a member of the Nazi party.

According to Dr. Michael J. Neufeld, Curator of the Smithsonian Institute's National Air and Space Museum in Washington, DC, regarding the NSDAP (Nationalsozialistische Deutsche Arbeiterpartei, or the National Socialist German Workers' Party aka the "Nazi" Party) however:

> It was a mass totalitarian party with over 12 million members, if memory serves. Until 1943 or 1944, however, the Weimar-era law that barred members of the armed forces from belonging to political parties remained in effect. That did not stop numerous members of the Wehrmacht (armed forces) from being Nazi enthusiasts, including in all probability Friedrich Steinhoff. His brother (Dr. Ernst) was a member and enthusiast.

7. At the end of World War II it was genuinely believed by certain Allied intelligence agencies that a fleet of German U-boats and surface ships may have ferried high ranking Nazi officials to secret bases at distant, discreet locations around the world, as Germany's capitulation grew imminent. Oberleutnant zur See, Heinz Schaffer, Commander of the Type VIIC U-boat *U-977*, who surrendered his boat at Mar del Plata, Argentina, on August 17, 1945 more than three months after Germany's surrender, was later accused by his Allied interrogators of ferrying Hitler to a secret German base in South America or Antarctica (one *Boston Post* newspaper headline of May 18, 1945 was entitled "Big Hunt on for Hitler in U-Boat").

   According to the French press (but never confirmed), in late September of 1946, nearly a year and a half after Germany's surrender, at least one German U-boat had still allegedly been operating near Tierra del Fuego, off the coast of the tip of South America. *France Soir* and *Agence France Presse* reported that the Icelandic whaling-ship "*Juliana*" had been stopped and boarded by Officers and crewmen from a large German submarine near Malvinas (now Falkland) Island, and according to Captain Hekla, were paid in American currency for a share of her fresh provisions. The renegade U-boat allegedly departed after advising Captain Hekla of the location of a large school (pod) of whales, which the *Juliana* later located in the area designated by the U-boat's Commander. Were there actually German U-boats operating in the Antarctic area more than a year after Germany's surrender, and if so, where were they getting their fuel, spare parts, provisions and other logistical supplies so long after the end of the war? Was there actually some remote secret German base from which such boats were operating? Modern research casts doubt on the veracity of the *France Soir* story, particularly of the existence of an Icelandic whaling ship *Juliana* and her alleged Captain named "Hekla."

During World War I, in 1915 the German cruiser S.M.S. *Dresden* explored the coast of South America and Tierra del Fuego, at the tip of South America, searching for hidden coves, passages and anchorages that could be exploited by Kaiserliche Marine warships operating in that area. It is also known that prior to the outbreak of World War II, German Kriegsmarine vessels including the D.K.M. *Schlesien* and D.K.M. *Schleswig-Holstein* conducted alleged "training cruises" to refresh German intelligence on those Unterschlupf-Platze (hiding-places) or so-called "U-Platze" along the South American Coast. Many of the Kriegsmarine's charted U-Platze were located in what the Germans called Feuerland or "fire-land" (Patagonia and Tierra del Fuego).

Between December of 1946 and March of 1947 the U.S. Navy dispatched three (3) battle groups including some 4,700

U.S. military personnel under command of Admiral Richard E. Byrd, for the officially reported purpose of "testing American military equipment in cold weather conditions." Because it appeared to many involved in the operation that significantly more "searching" was conducted rather than "testing," however, some have speculated that there was another, more secret reason for the operation.

It has been rumored that the operation, code-named "High-Jump" was actually mobilized to search the coast of Antarctica and Tierra del Fuego, for suspected secret "Nazi escape bases," none of which were ever located. Note: It was later learned that following the end of the war, Organization "Odessa" a group allegedly organized by a number of high-ranking Officers from Germany's former elite Schutzstaffeln (protection squadron) "SS" divisions (Odessa was an acronym for "Organization der ehemaligen SS-Angehorigen," or "Organization of former SS members"), had smuggled numerous Nazi war criminals to certain safe relocation areas in several South American countries, where they ultimately avoided prosecution at the Nuremberg Trials. It is known that incalculable millions of dollars in gold, jewels, works of art and other treasures were plundered from conquered nations by German forces during World War II, and have yet to be accounted for, some of which might have been used to finance the operations of Odessa.

8. Kapitanleutnant Johann-Heinrich Fehler's account of the sleepless night he spent in the Suffolk County "Charles Street Jail" in Boston, raises several unanswered questions that lurk within the pages of the many U.S. Navy records regarding the date(s) of his surrender, and the details of his whereabouts during his captivity under U.S. custody. Several of the deck-logs of the U.S. Navy and Coast Guard warships involved in the surrender of the German U-boats at Portsmouth, New Hampshire, and

other official records, contain a number of obvious discrepancies regarding the particular dates and times of certain related events that took place during the month of May 1945. Most U.S. Navy records indicate that Commander Fehler's boat, the *U-234* did not enter the harbor at Portsmouth until May 19th 1945, however, that is the same day that Commander Steinhoff was allegedly found mortally injured from an alleged self-inflicted wound, in his cell at the Charles Street Jail.

It is known that Commander Fehler and a number of his Officers and crewmen had been removed from the *U-234* and transferred to Portsmouth by the U.S. Coast Guard cutter *Argo* prior to the arrival of the *U-234* at the Portsmouth Navy Base, but had he been transferred to Boston on the 18th of May rather than the 19th? Was Commander Fehler mistaken about the identity of the other U-boat crew held in the Charles Street Jail on the evening that he and his crew were interned there, or are the official U.S. Navy records inaccurate? It is known that no other German U-boat commander died while in custody at the Charles Street Jail, so did Commander Fehler fabricate his account of those events?

Many who knew Commander Fehler described him as a highly educated, respected and honorable man, and a propensity to make up such a fabrication would not appear to have been within his character. Since the Suffolk County Coroner's records regarding the autopsy of Commander Steinhoff, and the U.S. Navy's Judge Advocate General's "Court of Inquiry" into the circumstances surrounding the death of Commander Steinhoff, are allegedly "missing and presumed lost," even the exact date when Commander Steinhoff was allegedly found bleeding in his cell, is open to genuine dispute. Commander Fehler's detailed recollection of those events, however, bear strong and convincing evidence that he was present in the Charles Street

Jail at the time that Commander Steinhoff was held there, and barring the production of certain "missing documents" by the U.S. Navy, Army and certain intelligence agencies within the federal government, this mystery may never be solved.

9. "Operation (aka Project) Paperclip" (originally called "Operation Overcast"), was the code-name for the American race to capture Germany's top scientists, technicians and engineers who were working on the development of the Third Reich's secret weapons development projects. The United States and Britain in particular, raced to beat the former Soviet Union in capturing Germany's top scientists, weapons, prototypes, plans and blueprints from occupied Europe in the weeks and months following the Axis surrender. Their successes and failures in that race played a large part in setting the stage for the protracted Cold War struggle that followed.

10. Ernst A. Steinhoff was born the son of Ludwig and Augusta Steinhoff in Treysa, Germany on February 11, 1908. Ernst Steinhoff had two younger brothers, Friedrich who was born in 1909, and Ludwig who was born in or about 1912. Ernst Steinhoff received his Master of Science degree, summa cum laude, and his Doctor of Engineering degree, cum laude, from the Darmstadt Institute of Technology in Darmstadt, Germany. In 1935 Dr. Steinhoff married Hildegard Madee, and they had seven children including sons: Hans, Ralph and Riner; and daughters: Hanelore, Monika, Gisela and Astrid.

    In 1935 Dr. Steinhoff set the world's record for solo long distance cross-country sail-plane (glider) flight of 314 miles, after which he was bestowed the honorary rank of "Flight Captain" with the German air force (Luftwaffe) for his flight achievements. Dr. Steinhoff taught aeronautical engineering at the Polytechnic Institute, Bad Frankenhausen, Germany, from 1936 to 1939, and conducted experimental work in aerodynamics, flight mechanics and airborne electronics equipment at the Aeronautical Research Institute at Darmstadt, Germany. He later became Director of Flight Mechanics, Ballistics, Guidance and Control and Instrumentation at the secret German Rocket Research Center at Peenamunde, Germany, on the Baltic Sea coast, where he served from July 1st 1939 to the Spring of 1945.

After accepting an invitation in 1945 to travel to the United States under "Operation Paperclip" Dr. Steinhoff continued his research as Section Chief in charge of the Steering Section of U.S. Army's Ordnance Research and Development Division at Fort Bliss, Texas, from 1945 to 1950. During that period, Dr. Steinhoff spent considerable time at White Sands Missile Range in Alamogordo, New Mexico, acting as head of the missile Guidance and Control group during many of the test firings of captured German V-2/A4 rockets. On May 29, 1947, he was in charge of the guidance systems of a modified, two-stage V-2 designated "Hermes II" (RTV-A-6) for testing of new top-secret ramjet technology, when he averted a near disaster when the rocket flew Southwest rather than its intended Northern trajectory. Steinhoff decided not to destroy the errant missile, hoping it would clear El Paso, and Juarez, Mexico, just across the Rio Grande River. His calculation paid off when the rocket crashed into a desolate area near a cemetery, a mile and a half South of Juarez, narrowly missing a shed filled with explosives stored by a Mexican mining company (the missile reached an apogee of 31 miles/50 km, and traveled 47 miles to the SSW of its launch site). Had the rocket been destroyed over a populated area like El Paso, the potential for civilian casualties would have been significant. From 1950 to 1954 Dr. Steinhoff was later appointed to Scientific Advisor on Guided Missiles and became Scientific Advisor to the Commander at the Holloman Air Force Base. Later Dr. Steinhoff was appointed as Technical Director of the Air Force Missile Development Center. After seven years of private service to the aerospace industry, Dr. Steinhoff returned to Holloman AFB as Chief Scientist of the Air Force Missile Development Center from 1963 to 1970.

After his retirement Dr. Steinhoff served an extended term as Director of the New Mexico Research Institute. He was a fellow of the Institute of Electric and Electronic Engineers and was inducted into the International Space Hall of Fame in 1979. Dr. Steinhoff passed away on Wednesday, December 2nd 1987. His funeral service was conducted by Rev. W.W. Fountain at the Hamilton Chapel in Alamogordo on December 6th 1987, followed by internment at Monte Vista Cemetery. During his life Dr. Steinhoff was one of the leading pioneers in the development of submarine launched missiles, and the United States' ballistic missile and space programs, and his great legacy will be valued by many generations to come (Taken in part from the obituaries of Dr. Ernst A. Steinhoff on December 4, 1987).

Acknowledgments

I am indebted to many people for their kind and generous assistance in researching and documenting this previously untold chapter in naval history. In particular, I would like to thank the late Jim Fahey, formerly the Archivist and Curator aboard the U.S. Navy Shipbuilding Museum, U.S.S. *Salem* (*CA-139*), at Quincy, Massachusetts; Author and Naval Historian, Professor, Dr. Jurgen Rohwer of Weinstadt, Germany; Curator, Mr. Horst Bredow and Kriegsmarine Historian and Author, Mr. Jak P. Mallmann-Showell at the U-Boot-Archiv at Cuxhaven-Altenbruch, Germany; Senior Archivist, the late Bernard Cavalcante at the U.S. Naval Historical Center in Washington, DC; Commander, C. Roger Wallin U.S.N.R. (Ret.) Combat Systems Department: U.S. Naval Undersea Warfare Center, Newport, Rhode Island; Dr. Michael J. Neufeld, Curator of the Space History Division of the Smithsonian Institute's National Air and Space Museum in Washington, DC; Archivist, Barry Zerby, of the Modern Military Records: Textual Archives Division of the National Archives at College Park, Maryland; Naval Historian and Author, Mr. Charles Dana Gibson; Myron "Zeke" Blahy, the American representative of the U-Boot Archiv; Mr. Harry Cooper, President of Sharkhunters International; Oceanographer, Biologist, Diver and Author, Mr. Henry "Hank" Keatts; Daughter and son-in-law of Dr. Ernst Steinhoff, Mrs. Monika Steinhoff-O'Friel and Mr. Daniel J. O'Friel, Esquire; Widow of Kapitanleutnant Friedrich Steinhoff, the late Ilse Steinhoff; Son of Kapitanleutnant Friedrich Steinhoff, Dr. Frank Steinhoff; U.S. Navy Captain (Ret.), Jerry Mason; former Oberfunkmaat (Radioman 2nd Class) aboard the *U-873*, the late Georg Seitz; Curator of the New Mexico Museum of Space History at Alamogordo, New Mexico, Mr. George House; Portsmouth (New Hampshire) Athenaeum Archive Library, Researcher & Archivist, Ms. Ursula Wright, and Head Librarian, Mr. Tom Hardiman; Rio Grande Historical Collections at New Mexico State University, Researcher, Mr. Dennis Daily; Portsmouth (New Hampshire) Naval Shipyard Public Affairs officials: Mr. Alan M. Robinson and Ms. Jan Hussey; Portsmouth Naval Shipyard Museum Archivist James Dolph, and Assistant Archivist Walter Ross; the late Volkmar Konig, former Fahnrich (Midshipman) aboard the U-boat *U-99* under Germany's top U-boat ace of W.W.II, Korvettenkapitan Otto Kretschmer; Colonel Frank E. Wismer, III (Chaplain) 94th Regional Readiness Command, U.S. Army Reserve, stationed at Fort Devens, Ayer, Massachusetts; David Guaraldi, Senior New Technology Specialist at Cognex Corp. of Natick, Massachusetts; Engineer and diver, Peter Kerrebrock, of Draper Labs, Inc. (formerly with the U.S.N. Undersea Warfare Center at Newport, Rhode Island); Diver and Naval and Maritime Historian, Chris Hugo; Former Marine Guard at the Portsmouth Naval Prison, the late Fred Flammini; Former Nurse/Receptionist at the Massachusetts General Hospital, Mrs. Rita (Rand) Conroy; Mr. David Rand; Captain (MC) USN (Ret.) and Medical Examiner, James R. Armstrong, M.D.; Mr. Charles Gundersen; German/English Translators, Ms. Amy O'Brien & the late Dr. Chester E. Claff, Jr.; Proofreader Grace Peirce; Photographer, Mr. Richard "Dick" Parnham; Dr. David B. Tanguay; Dr. Ernst O. Krause, President of EOK Technology, Inc, of Emerson, NJ; Martha's Vineyard Historian, Peter Colt Josephs, Cape Cod Maritime Historian Richard Weckler, and to my late parents, Judge (Ret.) James R. Lawton (10/20/25-03/20/07), and Jeanne G. Lawton (10/09/27-11/25/10).

Bibliography

Books

Blair, Clay. *Hitler's U-Boat War: The Hunters 1939-1942*. New York, NY: Random House, 1996.

Blair, Clay. *Hitler's U-Boat War: The Hunted 1942-1945*. New York, NY: Random House, 1998.

Botting, Douglas. *The Seafarers: The U-Boats*. Alexandria, VA: Time-Life Books, 1979.

Browning, Robert M. Jr., *U.S. Merchant War Casualties of World War II*. Annapolis, MD: Naval Institute Press, 1996.

Busch, Rainer and Roll, Hans-Joachim. *German U-Boat Commanders of World War II: A Biographical Dictionary*. Annapolis, MD: Naval Institute Press, 1999.

Compton-Hall, Richard. *Submarine Versus Submarine: The Tactics and Technology of Underwater Confrontation*. New York, NY: Orion Books, 1988.

Darren Court and the White Sands Missile Range Museum. *Images of America: White Sands Missile Range*. Charleston, SC: Arcadia Publishing. Charleston, 2009.

Engelmann, Joachim. *V1: The Flying Bomb*. Atglen, PA: Schiffer Publishing Ltd., 1992.

Engelmann, Joachim. *V2: Dawn of the Rocket Age*. Atglen, PA: Schiffer Publishing Ltd., 1992.

Fahey, James C. *The Ships and Aircraft of the United States Fleet, Second War Edition*, New York, NY: Gemsco, Inc. 1944.

Ford, Brian. *German Secret Weapons: Blueprint for Mars*. New York, NY: Ballantine Books. 1969.

Franklin, Bruce P. *The Buckley-Class Destroyer Escorts*. Annapolis, MD Naval Institute Press, 1999.

Friedman, Norman. *U.S. Destroyers*. Annapolis, MD: Naval Institute Press, 1982.

Friedman, Norman. *U.S. Small Combatants*. Annapolis, MD: Naval Institute Press, 1987.

Gander, Terry. *Germany's Guns 1939-45*. Wiltshire, England: The Crowood Press, Ltd., 1998.

Garlinski, Joseph. *Hitler's Last Weapons: The Underground War Against the V-1 and V-2*. Great Britain: Julian Friedmann Publishers Ltd., 1978.

Gentile, Gary. *Track of the Gray Wolf: U-Boat Warfare on the U.S. Eastern Seaboard 1942-1945*. New York, NY: Avon Books, 1989.

Gibson, James Norris. *The History of the U.S. Nuclear Arsenal*. Greenwich, CT: Brompton Books 1989.

Griehl, Manfred. *Luftwaffe Over America: The Secret Plans to Bomb the United States in World War II*. Mechanicsburg, PA: Stackpole Books, 2004.

Hadley, Michael L. *U-Boats Against Canada*. Montreal, Canada: McGill-Queen's University Press, 1985.

Holsken, Dieter. *V-Missiles of the Third Reich: The V-1 and V-2*. Hong Kong: Monogram Aviation Publications. 1994.

Hinkle, David Randall; Caldwell, Harry H.; and Johnson, Arne C. (Naval Submarine League) *United States Submarines*. China: Barnes & Noble Books. 2002.

Horton, Edward. *The Illustrated History of the Submarine*. Garden City, NY: Doubleday & Company, Inc. 1974.

Jacobsen, Annie. *Operation Paperclip: The Secret Intelligence Program that Brought Nazi Scientists to America*. New York, NY: Little, Brown and Company, 2014.

Jordan, Roger W. *The World's Merchant Fleets 1939*. Annapolis, MD: Naval Institute Press, 1999.

Keatts, Henry C. and Farr, George C., *U-Boats, Volume 3: Diving Into History*. Houston, TX: Pisces Books, 1994.

Kopenhagen, Wilfred. *The V1 And Its Soviet Successors*. Atglen, PA: Schiffer Military/Aviation History, 2000.

Lightbody, Andy and Poyer, Joe. *Submarines: Hunter/Killers & Boomers*. New York, NY: Beekman House, 1990.

Miller, David. U-Boats: *An Illustrated History of the Raiders of the Deep*. Washington, D.C.: Pegasus Publishing, 2000.

Milner, Marc. *The U-Boat Hunters: The Royal Canadian Navy and the Offensive Against German Submarines*. Annapolis, MD: Naval Institute Press, 1994.

Moffat, Alexander W. Capt. USNR (Ret.). *A Navy Maverick Comes of Age, 1939-1945*. Wesleyan University Press. Middleton, CT. 1977.

Morison, Samuel Eliot. *The Two-Ocean War: A Short History of the United States Navy in the Second World War*. Boston, MA: Little Brown and Company. 1963.

Neufeld, Michael J. *The Rocket and the Reich: Peenemunde and the Coming of the Ballistic Missile Era*. Cambridge, MA: Harvard University Press. 1995.

Niestle, Axel. *German U-Boat Losses During World War II: Details of Destruction*. Annapolis, MD: Naval Institute Press, 1998.

Rohwer, Jurgen. *Axis Submarine Successes. 1939-1945*. Annapolis, MD: Naval Institute Press, 1983.

Rohwer, Jurgen & Hummelchen, Gerhard. *Chronology of War at Sea, 1939-1945: The Naval History of World War II*. Annapolis, MD: Naval Institute Press, 1992.

Roscoe, Theodore, *United States Destroyer Operations of World War II*. Annapolis, MD: Naval Institute Press, 1953.

Roscoe, Theodore. *United States Submarine Operations in World War II*. Annapolis, MD., U.S. Naval Institute 1949.

Rossler, Eberhard. *The U-Boat: The Evolution and Technical History of German Submarines*. Annapolis, MD: Naval Institute Press, 1981.

Sellwood, A.V. *The Warring Seas*. London, England: Tandem Publishing Co. Ltd., 1956.

Scalia, Joseph M. *Germany's Last Mission to Japan: The Final Voyage of U-234*. Annapolis, MD: Naval Institute Press, 2000.

Schaffer, Heinz. *U-Boat 977*. William Kimber and Co. Ltd., London, England, 1952.

The Illustrated Encyclopedia of 20th Century Weapons and Warfare: Volume 1, A1/AMX. New York, NY: Columbia House 1977, pages 3 to 6.

The Illustrated Encyclopedia of 20th Century Weapons and Warfare: Volume 3, Avro 504/Berserk. New York, NY: Columbia House 1977, pages 257 to 263.

Van Zwienen, John. *Pivot*. New York, NY: Jove Publishing (ISBN: 051505495X), 1980.

White, John F.. *U-Boat Tankers 1941-45: Submarine Suppliers to Atlantic Wolf Packs*. Annapolis, MD: Naval Institute Press, 1998.

Williamson, Gordon. *Wolf Pack: The Story of the U-Boat in World War II*. Oxford, UK: Osprey Publishing, 2005.

Wynn, Kenneth. *U-Boat Operations of the Second World War, Volume 1: Career Histories, U-1 to U-510*. Annapolis, MD: Naval Institute Press, 1997.

Wynn, Kenneth, *U-Boat Operations of the Second World War, Volume 2: Career Histories, U-511 to UIT25*. Annapolis, MD: Naval Institute Press, 1998.

Other Published Sources

Alamogordo (NM) *Daily News*. Obituary of Dr. Ernst A. Steinhoff, December 4, 1987.

France Soir (magazine): "German Submarines in South America" (report on *Agence France Presse* article of 25 September 1946) circa September or October 1946.

Gray, Charlie. *Surrender at Sea*: A compilation of the stories of the surrender of the Nazi submarines as presented over WHEB Portsmouth, New Hampshire (for Colonial Laundry). McCandlish. circa 1945.

Missile RANGER: Published in the Interests of Personnel at White Sands Missile Range, Volume 37- Number 34. Steinhoff, Wagner to Hall of Fame (by Jim Eckles), August 24, 1984.

Sharkhunters magazine. "A Few Words About Hydrogen Peroxide." KTB # 168. May 2003.

Sharkhunters magazine. "From Naval Aviator to Submariner" (KL Paul Just) by Chuck Myles. KTB #177.June 2004.

Sharkhunters magazine. "U-Boat Rockets" by Chuck Myles. KTB # 199, page 42. May 2007.

Spark, Nick T., "Battle Stations Missile!" *Naval History* magazine, U.S. Naval Institute, Annapolis, MD, August 2003.

Stoelzel, Heinz. Die deutschen Raketen-U-Boote: Die ersten Erprobungen auf U 511 in der Ostsee. Schiff und Zeit 16, Cuxhaven, Germany 1982.

The Atlantic Monthly. "Found Object. Hitler's "Amerikabomber": The Idea of Flying Planes Into Skyscrapers Didn't Originate with al-Qaeda." (Dieter Wulf) page 41, May 2004.

The Boston Globe. "Captured U-boat Crew in Boston." May 11, 1945.

The Boston Globe. May 20, 1945.

The Boston Post, Allen, Lester. "Big Hunt on for Hitler in U-Boat." May 18, 1945.

The Dolphin: Serving the Best Submarine Homeport in the World. Volume 22, No. 35. By Lt. Edward Lundquist (Public Affairs Officer Submarine Group Two "What if the Germans had Listened to U-boat Skipper ?" September 30, 1983.

The New York Times, "How Marshal Goering Drew a Bead on New York." Tuesday, April 2, 1946.

Unpublished Sources

Army Service Forces: Headquarters First Service Command. Letter of Colonel (INF) A.J. Lamereaux, Chief Provost Marshal Branch, Security and Intelligence Division, Subject: Transfer of German Navy Prisoners of *U-873*. SPBIP 383.6. May 21, 1945.

CBS News: *World War II With Walter Cronkite* "Air War Over Europe: Episode IV: Guided Missiles" 1983.

Death Certificate of Friedrich Steinhoff, City of Boston, May 19, 1945.

Department of the Navy, Naval Historical Center. Disposition of German Submarines in U.S. Custody at the End of World War II. Date Unknown.

Department of the Navy, Naval Historical Center. Letter of Bernard F. Cavalcante, Head, Operational Archives Branch, to Mr. Charles Backus, 5750/ Ser AR/02816. Reply to Request for Information on U-873 dated May 20, 1998.

Des Führers/Befehlshaber der Unterseeboote (F.d.U./B.d.U.) War Diary and War Standing Orders of Commander in Chief, Submarines: 16-30 November 1942. PG30313b, courtesy of the U-boat Archive.

E-mail from U.S. Navy Captain Jerry Mason (Ret.) to author Paul M. Lawton on July 4, 2003.

Formerly Classified May 1st to May 31st 1945 Deck Log Entries of U.S.C.G.C. *Argo* (*CGC-100*).

Formerly Classified May 1st to May 31st 1945 Deck Log Entries of U.S.S. *Otter* (*DE-210*).

Formerly Classified May 1st to May 31st 1945 Deck Log Entries of U.S.S. *Sutton* (*DE-771*).

Formerly Classified United States Marine Corps Marine Barracks, Navy Yard, Portsmouth, New Hampshire. Letter from F.G. Patchen, Subject: Surrender of German U-boats *805*, *873* and *1228*; report of activities of Marines of this command in connection therewith. 17 May 1945.

Formerly Confidential Basic Personnel Records (Alien Enemy or Prisoner of War) information sheets, photographs and fingerprints of the Officers and crewmen of the *U-873*.

Formerly Confidential Chief of Naval Operations (CNO) and Commander-in-Chief (CominCh) Directives regarding the "Procedure for Handling Prisoners of War" date unknown.

Formerly Confidential Facts and Discussions of Facts Regarding Allegations of Serious Irregularities Involving the Handling of the Prisoners, Extensive Looting by Officers and Men Attached to the Naval Prison, Drunkenness Amongst the Guards on the

Submarine, Loss of Valuable Intelligence Documents and Poor Security Measures in Connection with the Receipt of German Prisoners and U-Boats at the Navy Yard, Portsmouth, New Hampshire. 6 03301. Declassified Authority NN0803073 date 2/24/92.

Formerly Confidential Report on Events at Portsmouth Navy Yard in Connection with the Surrender of German Submarines *U-234, U-805, U-873* and *U-1228*. from Jack H. Alberti to Capt. John L. Riheldaffer, USN (Ret.). 22 May 1945.

Formerly Secret German Transcript of the Discussion of December 9, 1944 Concerning the Use of the A4 from the Sea, Towed by U-boats.

Formerly Secret Op-16-Z: Preliminary Report on the Interrogation of Survivors from *U-546* Sunk on 24 April 1945. 3 May 1945 (5 pages).

Formerly Secret Op-16-Z: Report on Interrogation of the Crew of *U-873* which Surrendered to the USS *Vance* on 11 May 1945 in Position 35 degrees-45'N, 42 degrees-31'W. (5 pages).

Formerly Secret Secretary of the Navy/Chief of Naval Operations correspondence (Record Group 80) "Irregularities connected with the handling of surrendered German submariners and prisoners of war at the Navy Yard, Portsmouth, NH," 19 June 1945.

Formerly Secret U.S. Navy Office of Naval Intelligence Letter Report: United States Naval Technical Mission to Europe: Report on Interrogation of Dr. (Ernst) Steinhot [*sic*] by Dr. E.H. Krause and F/L H.R. Brock on 16-18 May 1945.

Formerly Secret U.S. Navy Office of Naval Intelligence Letter Report: United States Naval Technical Mission to Europe: Interrogation of General Dornberger at Parten Kirchen, Germany on 15 May 1945 by Dr. E.H. Krause and Lt. (jg) P.W. Wilkerson, (USNR).

Formerly Top Secret Ultra Report included in the U.S. Navy's World War II Op-20-G Final Report Series on the Battle of the Atlantic. Volume II SRH-008 (date unknown).

Geneva Convention: Articles of the Regulations annexed to the Hague Convention respecting the laws and customs of war on land, and captured enemy, dated October 18, 1907.

Interviews of Volkmar Konig regarding conversations with Ilse Steinhoff, 2001 & 2002.

Letter from Colonel Frank E. Wismer, III (Chaplain) 94th Regional Readiness Command, U.S. Army Reserve, to author Paul M. Lawton dated 27 October 2005;

Letter from Dr. Frank Steinhoff to author, Paul M. Lawton dated November 4, 2002.

Letter from Dr. Frank Steinhoff to author, Paul M. Lawton dated January 8, 2003.

Letter from Dr. Frank Steinhoff to author, Paul M. Lawton dated January 10, 2003.

Letter from Dr. Michael J. Neufeld, Curator of the Space History Division of the Smithsonian Institute's National Air and Space Museum in Washington, DC, to the author, Paul M. Lawton dated September 2, 2004.

Letter from James R. Armstrong, M.D., Capt. (MC) USN (Ret.) Diplomate American Board of Surgery. April 29, 2003.

Letter from Kapitanleutnant Johann-Heinrich Fehler (Hamburg) to Harry Cooper (President of Sharkhunters International), dated September 9, 1985.

Letter from Kapitanleutnant Johann-Heinrich Fehler (Hamburg) to Wolfgang Hirschfeld (Plon, Germany), 3 February 1981.

Letter from Kapitan zur See Friedrich Grade, former Chief Engineer aboard the *U-96*, to Dr. Frank Steinhoff dated January 8, 2003.

Letter from Philip K. Lundebuerg, Curator Emeritus at the Smithsonian Institute, regarding "Operation Teardrop Revisited," to Dr. Dean Allard, Director of the Naval Historical Center at Washington, D.C., 23 November 1993.

Letter from Philip K. Lundebuerg, Curator Emeritus at the Smithsonian Institute, regarding "Operation Teardrop

Revisited," to Professor Timothy Runyan of the Department of History at Cleveland State University. 20 November 1993.

Letter from Professor, Dr. Jurgen Rohwer, dated April 30, 2003.

Letter from the Commanding Officer of the U.S. Marine Corps Marine Barracks, Navy Yard, Portsmouth, New Hampshire to the Commandant of the USMC, Washington, D.C., Subject: Surrender of German U-Boats *805*, *873*, and *1228*; report of activities of marines of this command in connection therewith. 17 May 1945.

Letter from Volkmar Konig to author, Paul M. Lawton regarding conversations with Dr. Frank Steinhoff in November of 2002.

Notes from Interview with Stabmaschinist Heinz Reise, Former Engineering Officer of the *U-511* and the *UIT-24*. Interview Conducted at the Home of Charles Dana Gibson, Hillsdale, New York on November 3rd 1971.

Phone interview by author, Paul M. Lawton with David Rand regarding the recollections of his sister, Mrs. Rita (Rand) Conroy.

Phone interview by author, Paul M. Lawton with Fred Flammini, former U.S. Marine guard at the Portsmouth, New Hampshire Naval Prison.

Smithsonian Institute, National Air and Space Museum: Space History Division. Rockets and Missiles 1995-2000.

Video taped reproduction of original German celluloid 16mm film entitled *The Secret Military Operation of the Peenemunde Army Post: Underwater Shooting of Rocket Mortars*, filmed on the Baltic Sea off the coast Germany's secret rocket research base.

NOTE

Please excuse the occasional grammatical and misspelling errors in the foregoing document, as this is not a final draft. This story is still being researched, and is updated periodically as new witnesses are located and interviewed, and as new documentation and evidence is uncovered. As a result, please check the revised copyright dates to insure that you have an updated copy. All misspellings, grammatical errors, and historical inaccuracies from official government records and other cited sources have been set forth in this account, verbatim. Every effort has been made to make note of those errors however, and to set forth the appropriate corrections.

Copyright Warning

Copyright Certificates of Registration #:
TXu 1-028-192 (11/06/01); TXu 1-078-072 (08/26/02);
TXu 1-101-555 (05/20/03); TXu 1-167-693 (02/09/04);
TXu 1-317-687 (05/08/06).

*Revised To Date/Time: 02/19/15 @ 10:05 EST

Naval History/Non-Fiction

ISBN: 978-1-938394-39-3

Researched, Prepared and Published by Author:
Paul M. Lawton, Esquire
Naval Historian
The Lawyers' Building
157 Belmont Street
Brockton, MA 02301-5107
United States of America
Cell Phone: (508) 580-8300
Fax: (508) 584-8524
E-Mail: paulmlawton@yahoo.com